To our darling Holly
from Mom & Dad
June, 1985

Also by Dimetra Makris

FIRST PRIZE COOKBOOK

with Diane Powell and David Dax

Dimetra Makris

First Prize Quilts

Simon and Schuster · New York

Copyright © 1984 by Dimetra Makris
All rights reserved
including the right of reproduction
in whole or in part in any form
Published by Simon and Schuster
A Division of Simon & Schuster, Inc.
Simon & Schuster Building
Rockefeller Center
1230 Avenue of the Americas
New York, New York 10020
SIMON AND SCHUSTER and colophon are registered
trademarks of Simon and Schuster.
Designed by Elizabeth Woll

Manufactured in the United States of America

10   9   8   7   6   5   4   3   2   1

Library of Congress Cataloging in Publication Data
Makris, Dimetra.
    First prize quilts.

    Bibliography: p.
    Includes index.
    1. Quilting.   2. Quilts—United States.   I. Title.
TT835.M344   1984   746.9'7   84-5552
ISBN 0-671-46938-X

For my Father and Mother

ACKNOWLEDGMENTS

For their encouragement and support, I thank my parents.

A very special thank you to Julian Bach and Patricia Soliman, who helped bring the idea of this book to a reality.

I am grateful to Pamela Krauss for her constant, invaluable guidance and for her enthusiasm, understanding, and support. Without her the book would not have been as it is.

For his patience and excellent guidance, I thank Leon Morse.

Thank you to my brother Bill for being there and for excellent help with the photography.

For always listening and for sharing this dream, thank you to my very special friend, Susan Wolf Rifkin. Thanks to Irene Stein, who first mentioned quilts. To Susan Rodgers, thanks for her help. To Lynne Aikman, who wouldn't listen to excuses, thank you. For helping me reach this goal, my thanks to Edward Black.

So many individuals generously gave help and advice that it is impossible to list all of them, but I would like to publicly thank a few of them.

The staff and volunteers of the library of the Cooper-Hewitt Museum, and especially Margaret Luchars, provided invaluable aid during my research. Rosemary Frye Plakas of the Library of Congress extended her skilled assistance; her valuable contribution is greatly appreciated.

I am grateful to Peggy Gilfoy, of the textile department of the Indianapolis Museum of Art, and to Joanne Polster, librarian of the American Crafts Council, for their help. Both the New York office of the Embroiderers' Guild of America and the many chapter members throughout the county were extremely generous with their advice and assistance.

My special thanks to Alice Skarda, Denise Johnson of the Danville (Virginia) Public Library, Susan Murwin, and Hazel Carter for sharing their knowledge and time in helping with this book.

To Mr. and Mrs. DeLance Franklin, Sally Garoutte, Fay Goldey, Irene Goodrich, Deborah Kakalia, Marsha Melton, Betty Lou Pearson, Steve Pooch, and Marguerite Wiebusch, many thanks for their assistance.

My thanks to all of the state and county fair officials, the county extension agents, fellow home economists, and all those dedicated secretaries in offices around the country who helped so very much.

I am grateful to the many photographers, both professional and amateur, who contributed photographs.

To the quilters included in the book, many of whom have become friends across the miles, thank you for sharing so much.

To the many fine quilters who answered my queries but whom we could not include because of space limitations, thank you, each one of you.

And for all his infinite patience, I thank Clark.

CONTENTS

INTRODUCTION

*T*his book is for and about today's quilters. Too often collections such as this have looked to the past for excellence in the arts and in hand-crafted goods, neglecting the fine examples being created by modern artists and craftspeople.

Whether we consider the vast array of quilts and needlework produced today, the workmanship of contemporary handmade furniture, or even the revival of regional cooking and baking, we find artistry that is superior. This does not diminish the important contributions of artisans of the past, but rather reflects our intention to put the present in proper perspective.

I was pleasantly surprised by the high caliber of modern quilts, demonstrated even in the first endeavors of new quilters. Though this made selecting examples for this collection much harder, it was rewarding to see the care and technique these new quiltmakers apply to their work. Many of these young women and men had no history of quilting in their families; for many, quiltmaking skipped a generation or two before being revived by them. In some cases, these young quilters have taught their parents to quilt.

For many others, of course, quilting has long been a family tradition. But whether they are practicing a newfound art or the continuation of a tradition, each of the quilters represented here has added his or her personal touch to the finished work.

First Prize Quilts includes prizewinning quilts from state, county, local, and national competitions. These contests are as diversified as their titles: the National Quilters Association Quilt Show; the Quilting Society of America; the Annual Quilt Contest & Exhibition, sponsored by Dan River, Inc., and the Danville (Vir-

ginia) Public Library; the Annual Quilting Contest of the Pennsylvania Dutch Kutztown Folk Festival; the National Cranberry Quilt Patch Contest; the National Peanut and Fair Festival (Dothan, Alabama); as well as many state fairs and county fairs, the National Grange contest, the Santa Rosa show, and many, many more.

Within these contests are a growing number of categories. In addition to the obvious categories such as machine- or hand-pieced quilts, appliqué or patchwork submissions, there are classifications such as novelty, cross-stitched, baby or crib, cathedral, miniature, painted, smallest patchwork in cotton, liquid painting, embroidered. There are also separate categories in some contests for the type of quilt, such as sampler, medallion, and so forth. There are also awards, such as Best of Show, and in some cases, Most Popular of Show, often the most coveted prize, which is voted on by the viewing public rather than the official judges.

The intention of this book is to cover a cross section of quilt competitions and to include a wide variety of winners. There was no strict set of rules, except that each quilt be a first-prize winner. Represented are quilters who have been perfecting their skills for twenty, thirty, or even seventy years, as well as newcomers who entered their very first quilts in contests and came away with the top prizes.

Quilts of all materials, techniques, sizes, and design were considered. Some winners included in the book have taken prizes across the country and even internationally, others on a local or state level. It was difficult to select only one representative per state because of the volume of outstanding quilts submitted for inclusion. This collection can offer only a sprinkling of the delightful handiwork one can find throughout the country.

Many of these quilters belong to clubs or guilds or simply meet in each other's homes, while others quilt independently. Several of the prizewinners began by taking classes and are now themselves teachers. Some even have their own shops.

Over and over again, quilters spoke of their understanding families and supportive husbands and wives. Even in busy homes, the quilter somehow finds precious moments to work on a current project. Whether it be while waiting for her husband to finish the 6:00 A.M. milking or during those endless waits in chauffeuring children to one appointment after another, those skilled fingers make every spare minute count, with beautiful results.

Working on this book was a bit like having been invited into an exclusive and special society. The quilter's network is unique in that so many of these talented people know each other, either personally or by reputation. They gave generously of their time and information for this book. Many prizewinners, when contacted, would suggest the names of other winners for consideration in the book—even if only one could be selected for publication.

Though quilting is now hundreds of years old and designs may have changed or been added to or adapted, the spirit of quilting remains the same. It symbolizes a sharing of ideas and work, an exchange of knowledge, and most of all, encouragement among fellow craftspersons.

Chapter 1

QUILTING'S RICH HERITAGE

Quilting may have begun with an Egyptian queen's patchwork goatskin funeral tent (960 B.C.). Or the Chinese may have been the first to fashion padded patchwork clothing. Or the first quilted product might have been the Persian quilted carpet. But wherever it began, patchwork and quilting have had a long, colorful history.

Of course, today when we think of quilts we tend to identify them with the early-American variety brought over by the colonists as economic and physical necessities. These were the warm bedcovers as well as wall and window hangings used to ward off the bitter cold drafts of the harsh winters. The severe winters required that several quilts, sometimes as many as four or five per bed, be used during the coldest months. In rural communities, these conditions existed well into the twentieth century.

Quilting served another purpose—a social one—in the lives of the early settlers. Women exchanged pieces from their scrapbags, and, eventually, the quilting bee evolved as a communal activity or as an excuse for a get-together. Since the conventions of the time limited these women to their homes and churches, the quilting bee was a way around those restrictions. It is said that Susan B. Anthony found attentive audiences at quilting bees for some of her early lectures on woman suffrage.

Recently, the quilting bee has been revived in a variety of forms. Some of these quilters' groups begin as classes and gradually become a permanent group which meets regularly to quilt. Even in large cities professional business women and men with hectic schedules are finding quilting groups to be an antidote to the isolation of contemporary lifestyles. The quilter finds companionship, a common interest, and

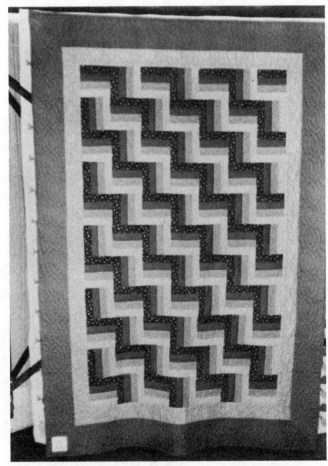

A popular early American design, the Vined Rail Fence *(Joyce Ganser)*

creative release that comes from doing something totally different from everyday work. Many women and men who had not even seen a patchwork piece

11

until a few years ago are now making and designing their own quilts.

Quilts today reflect the life of the quilter, just as they did many years ago. Album quilts often showed important events in the lives of a family. Nowadays, we find similar pieces recording a family history, or a family hobby or interest. Quilts with baseball, garden and flower, musical, and many other motifs represent personal memories of a family to be kept in a visual and lasting record that will be passed on to future generations. Other designs are of a political, historical, or religious nature. The recent spurt of renewed interest in quilts and quilting was in great part due to the Bicentennial celebration in 1976.

Similarly, much renewed interest in making a quilt as a church project or even in designing quilted vestments is evident today.

With the rediscovery of this country's quilting heritage have come rich discoveries in the variety of forms and styles of this native folk art. One recent area of interest is Southern quiltmakers. Susan Roach-Lankford has researched two groups of quilters in Louisiana, the Euro-American and the Afro-American, comparing traditions and the differences and similarities in these quilters and their work.

The Afro-American quilter and African textile influence on today's quilts has been the subject of Maude Wahlman's research. These quilts reflect a unique blend of African textile styles and quilting traditionally thought of as American. The designs combine color sense and rhythm for extraordinary visual effect. Today, these quilts are frequently not sewn in a precise manner, to resemble the earlier quilts—for example, stitches may be uneven and very large, as they were in earlier times out of economic necessity, since there was not much thread to work with. Early quilters frequently unwove fabric—old sacks, for example—to use the thread in piecing their quilts.

Often, early Afro-American quilts were done from freehand drawings and from appliqués cut from a variety of scrap fabric. Templates were not used, nor were the traditional quilting patterns. These quilts were (and are) made for family use, and so far as can be determined, were not exhibited or entered into fairs. The precision needed to stand up to that kind of judging is not part of these quilts. Rather these are simply remarkable examples of textile art—with strong roots in the ancestral country as well as definite American overtones.

Traditional bridal counterpane by Dorothy Sayre

L. Toomer's Cotton Leaf Quilt *from Georgia*

Rabbits and Hands, *by Sarah Mary Taylor, Mississippi*

Other kinds of distinctive quilts also play an important role in the history of this textile art. Mention Pennsylvania and one immediately thinks of Amish quilts, which, of course, have also been made and are currently made in many other Amish communities throughout the country, including large settlements in Indiana and Illinois. The designs of Amish quilts are usually geometric and nonrepresentational. The most impressive element in these quilts is the use of especially vivid colors in bold combinations. These colors represent an unusual statement of contrast with the simple environment that the sect lives and works in.

Amish patchwork designs are abstract, often developed around a central medallion such as a diamond. The quilting stitches, however, sometimes represent flowers or other recognizable shapes. Amish women did not appliqué their designs; rather, they let color and fine stitching define the outline and play of shapes.

Another quilt which is easily recognized is the Hawaiian design. Although it originated thousands of miles away, the popularity of this appliqué has spread across the country; fine examples can frequently be found in regional shows in all parts of the United States.

The recent revival in the popularity of quilts is evident in the number of museum exhibitions throughout the country. In addition, private industry has begun to help promote and sustain this valuable American folk art. The Quaker Oats Company has a quilt hanging in the chairman's boardroom that has many of the company's symbols worked into it. Mobil Oil Corporation recently presented a grant to the Continental Quilting Congress to support a quilt exhibit, and the Philip Morris Company commissioned regional artisans and craftspersons to produce a collection of their handiwork to be housed in its new Cabarrus County (North Carolina) facility. The highlight of this collection is a quilt measuring ten feet by thirty-eight feet, composed of three hundred and thirty-three traditional patterns in one-foot squares. Seven hundred different fabrics were used and fifty-three local quilters worked on the piece.

Though most quilters are assumed to have been women, there is a tradition throughout history of some men "dipping into" this reserve of domestic art. Many families worked on quilts as a group, with some

Jacky Dittmer's **Amish Quilt** *for America's Bicentennial*

14

Several traditional Hawaiian motifs are featured in Hazel Ferrell's Hawaiian Sampler

The Quaker Oats *quilt, designed by artist Edward Larson and quilted by Alice L. Dunsdon*

The Cabarrus Quilt, *designed for Philip Morris by Eugenia Balcells and produced by Maco Crafts, Inc.*

Simon & Schuster quilt

members cutting and others stitching. There are references to men signing their quilts in several books, and even Presidents Coolidge and Eisenhower worked at making quilts when they were youngsters. Today, many men have discovered this art form and are now becoming more active in displaying and entering their works in competition.

The quilts of the early pioneers were the visual record of the settling and development of the nation. Because they represent a period in our past, a time in our history, they have become an important part of the rediscovery of our heritage. The quilts being made today are a continuation of that pride in American tradition.

Chapter 2

STORING, DISPLAYING, AND CARING FOR QUILTED PIECES

*T*oday's quilts are tomorrow's heirlooms and should be cared for well. Some guidelines for the care of modern quilts follow. For antique quilts or damaged pieces, professional help should be sought.

STORAGE

All textiles should be stored clean and should be handled with spotlessly clean hands. Quilts should never be stored in plastic. They should be covered by a plain white cotton (or muslin) cloth or sheet. Any quilt or other textile stored for a considerable length of time should be rolled, not folded. If, however, that is not possible, it is best to take the quilt out and refold it from time to time so that excessive stress will not be placed on any particular part of the quilt.

Many quilters store their quilts on a spare bed, but good care includes keeping the quilt out of direct sunlight. Cooking and tobacco smoke can also damage delicate fabrics; exposed quilts should be protected from such fumes.

For preventing insect problems, mothballs are effective. Pennyroyal leaves (an herb found in many health food or natural goods stores) hung in double cheesecloth bags or in muslin bags are also effective in preventing damage by insects. Pennyroyal has a much less noticeable odor than mothballs, but must be replaced more frequently. Never place mothballs or pennyroyal directly on the fabric.

Textiles should be kept out of contact with wood surfaces. If they are stored in a drawer or trunk, Permalife paper or acid-free paper should be used to line all surfaces that come in contact with the quilts.

These papers can usually be found in photographic supply stores and art stores. UF–3 Plexiglas will prevent ultraviolet rays from harming small pieces that are framed and displayed. This can be found in art supply stores and can sometimes be special-ordered from a local hardware store.

Quilts should never be hung on wire hangers, and labels should not be stapled or pinned onto the fabric, as metal can oxidize and cause discolorations and stains.

All minor repairs on a handmade quilt should be hand sewn with thread that closely matches the fabric both in fiber content and color.

CLEANING

Many quiltmakers prefer to send their quilts to dry cleaners. Be sure that the firm is knowledgeable about the care of quilts.

Washing quilts at home is also common, particularly if the item is in constant use. Though machine washing on a gentle cycle is a general practice, it is not a good practice. Hand washing is preferable, but if that is not feasible, caution should be taken to use lukewarm or cold water and the lowest possible agitation cycle.

Before any wet cleaning of a quilt is considered, the quilt should be checked to determine if it is colorfast. A non-ionic detergent such as Orvus WA Paste, D.W. 300, Igepal or a very mild dishwashing detergent such as Ivory Liquid should be used. No soaps (such as Ivory Snow, Flakes, et cetera) should be used, because they will leave a film and can yellow white fabrics.

If possible, distilled or softened water should be used. Hard water is not recommended because it contains mineral deposits which can cause yellowing and staining and can, in time, break down the textile fibers. If it is difficult to use distilled or softened water, at least try to use them in the final rinse.

It is best to dry a quilt on a flat surface, rather than by hanging it from a clothesline. Also, if possible, it is best to squeeze excess water from a quilt; never wring the fabric. Clothes dryers are not recommended for drying quilts as they may cause shrinkage or fading.

Chlorine bleach should not be used to remove spots or whiten quilts. To brighten a white quilt, use only a 3 percent solution of hydrogen peroxide and rinse thoroughly. *Never* use peroxide on delicate or colored quilts.

DISPLAY

To hang a quilt, one of two methods may be used. The preferred one is to sew a strip of unsized cotton along the upper edge of the quilt. Next, fasten a band of Velcro to that strip. A piece of Velcro can then be attached to the wall and the quilt pressed against it to hang.

A second method is to make a sleeve of muslin, and baste it to the quilt with small stitches, penetrating the entire top of the quilt at the top edge. Through this sleeve a wooden or metal rod can be inserted and the quilt then hung from supports on the wall. The important features are that the stress be equally distributed over the quilt and that the wood or metal never come into direct contact with the fabric.

For special problems, professional advice should be sought. In many communities, the local museums have personnel trained in textile conservation. There are also a small but growing number of professionals who work independently on restoring textiles and helping with special problems.

There are many sources of information about the care and handling of quilts available throughout the country. Two excellent sources are *Consideration for the Care of Textiles and Costumes: A Handbook for the Non-Specialist,* by Harold F. Mailand, published by the Indianapolis Museum of Art; and the Textile Conservation Workshop, Main Street, South Salem, New York 10590.

Chapter 3

GENERAL QUILTING INSTRUCTIONS

ithout exception, the quilts considered for inclusion in this book are of the highest quality; elegantly designed, skillfully stitched, and masterfully pieced. They are representative of quilting at its very finest.

Many of these fine quilters have shared their piecing patterns and quilting designs, enabling the reader to recreate these lovely and intricate masterpieces. Instructions for many individual quilts accompany the designs. This chapter will provide guidelines and explain some of the terms used throughout the book and by quilters across the country.

TYPES OF QUILTS

Within the broad definition of patchwork quilts there are three basic types—pieced, appliquéd, and crazy.

Pieced quilts are made from materials cut into geometric shapes—such as squares, triangles, rectangles, or diamonds—which are sewn together in a pattern to form a larger block. Most pieced quilts are based on the block (or square) pattern. These blocks may all be of the same pattern or of two or more patterns alternated on the quilt top to give the desired overall effect. The blocks may be joined together to form the

Budding Star, *a pieced quilt, by Aileen Stannis*

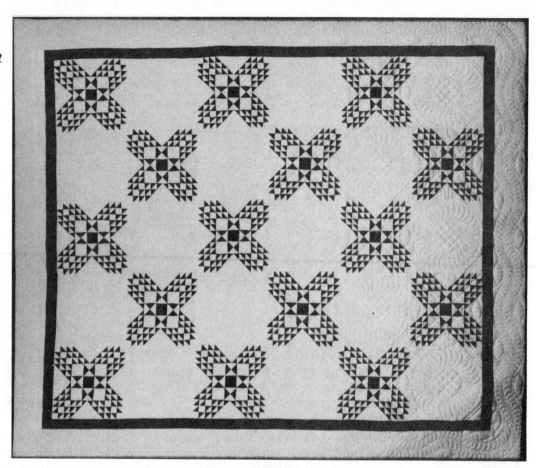

A variation of the eight-point star, Twinkling Star, *by Mrs. Jennings Davis*

total design, or they may be set together with strips of fabric.

One of the simplest pieced patterns is the eight-point star formed of diamond patches.

Appliquéd quilts are made by cutting a design from pieces of fabric, turning under the raw edges, and sewing this design onto a background fabric. This background can be a length of fabric or it can be separate blocks. An appliqué quilt can often be more time-consuming for several reasons: There are two layers to the quilt top; preparing the pieces for the appliqué requires skill in designing and placing of pieces; and frequently a basting process is needed before the actual stitching can be done. All these steps can be far more complicated than working with a single block design in a pieced quilt.

However, greater flexibility is the positive side of working on an appliqué quilt. The quilter is not necessarily bound by the geometric disciplines of piecing and has the freedom to make a simple shape or to develop an intricate, detailed, curving design.

Very often appliqué quilts are referred to as "show" quilts. Unlike the majority of pieced quilts, the appliqué quilts were not made for everyday use. Because of the cost of buying special fabrics to cut

into appliqué pieces (unlike the scrap fabric used for pieced and crazy quilts) and the need for large lengths of material for the background, they were intended primarily for special occasions.

Many more appliqué quilts have survived because of the fact that they were not used as everyday bedcovers. The real popularity of appliqué quilts began in the South, where the lady of the house, who had the time and could afford the costs, would make these rich handiworks, while the servants worked on the pieced quilts that were used daily.

Crazy quilts (the name is from an eighteenth-century term for fragmented formation of structure, as in "crazed glass") are considered by many to be the oldest form of patchwork. It evolved from the pioneer's necessity of using every precious scrap of material. When there wasn't enough fabric to cut even small repeat designs, the tiniest of scraps were pinned randomly on a backing material and then embellished with added embroidery or stitching around the edges of each piece. These were probably the quilts the early settlers made and used during their harsh winters in this country.

During the late 1800s and into the early twentieth century, there was a revival in making crazy quilts.

Appliquéd Balloons over Louisville, *by Imogene Lance*

The exquisite appliqué of Edrie Clifton's fanciful Courting Herons *won First Prize in the Dan River Quilt Contest*

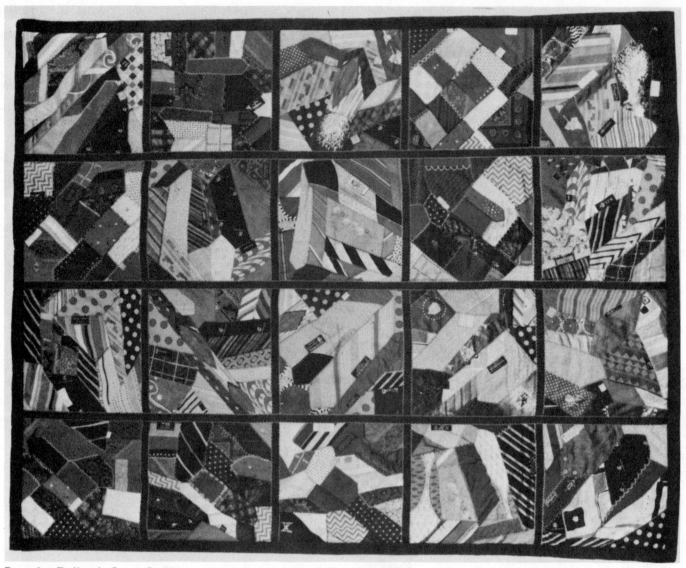

Dorothy Ballast's Crazy Quilt *is made entirely of friends' and family's neckties*

This version of the quilt is frequently referred to as the Victorian crazy quilt, because it was often found in the ornate, decorative parlor of that era. This new version was made of elegant fabrics, such as silks, brocades, and velvets, and in various bright colors. It was usually much smaller than most quilts and was used as a lap blanket or merely as a decorative throw in the parlor, rather than as a bedcover. Often scenes were painted on the patches, or pictures were reproduced by copying them in embroidery stitches. Many of these served nostalgic functions, as well, incorporating fabrics that were worn by family members and stitching important dates into the quilt.

In recent years, Victorian crazy quilts have lost favor and are often criticized for their excessive embellishment. However, they have their own charm, and many that have survived are special treasures for the families who own them. There are also delightful contemporary examples of this quilt style, and new quilters who aspire to make a crazy quilt should enjoy the flexibility that this method affords the beginner.

There are almost unlimited variations on these three basic quilting themes, and many quilts combine two or even all three techniques.

For example, some quilts are not quilted at all. Tied or tufted pieces (also known as comforters) may be pieced or appliquéd, but, instead of the fine overall quilting that secures the layers of most quilts, tied quilts are joined together by tufted knots, spaced at regular intervals across the quilt top, which pierce all three layers. This makes for a puffier, but less detailed bedcover.

Another quilting technique used to create a relief effect is the corded or "trapunto" quilting. A piece of loosely woven fabric is basted to the underside of the quilt top, then a design is sewn in two parallel rows of stitching and wool yarn is forced between the rows to form a raised design on the quilt top. Trapunto quilting was widely used in England and on the Continent during the seventeenth and eighteenth centuries to decorate petticoats, caps, and other garments, as well as to make counterpanes of exquisite beauty. Because it was meant to be decorative rather than functional, trapunto quilting was often done on delicate silks, satins, and velvets, and no batting was used between the layers of fabric. Trapunto is still used for decorative details on women's clothing.

Closely related to trapunto is stuffed work, in which selected areas of a quilt, generally appliquéd motifs such as fruits or flowers, are stuffed with loose pieces of wadding from the back. When these stuffed areas are surrounded with fine rows of quilting, they create a raised effect.

Yet another quilting technique is strip or Seminole quilting, the earliest method developed for stitching quilts by machine. These intricate geometric strips and zigzags have been a part of the Seminole tradition in quilts as well as in quilted clothing for many, many years.

These are just a very few of the host of methods that can be employed to assemble a quilt. Many of the most unique quilts being made today use very little traditional technique; often they combine conventional piecing and appliqué with such artistic techniques as silkscreening.

MAKING A QUILT

As in any new endeavor, patience and planning help to ensure successful results. There are many ways to make a quilt—the "English" system, strip patchwork, medallion patchwork, and others; the following is the traditional method based on blocks.

Selecting the Pattern and the Fabric

The first step toward making a quilt is to select a pattern. Whether it be a simple block pattern, a sampler, an appliqué, or any other design, it is important that you be aware of the steps involved. Advice abounds about not attempting a complicated pattern; yet some quilters attempt a difficult project on their first try and are pleased with the results. Know your capabilities and take it from there.

Soccer Balls, *a first-prize-winning tufted quilt by nine-year-old Danny Taylor*

Amelia Earhart *is an innovative quilt by Steve Stratakos combining a wide variety of materials.*

After deciding on a design, select the fabric. The material should be suitable for the pattern. Soft, closely woven fabric is usually a good choice because it is easy to handle and will hold its shape. Avoid fabrics that are harsh or rough, as well as cloth that has an open weave or is easily stretched. If you are using scrap materials, be careful to choose pieces that are not too worn. Some good choices of fabrics include broadcloth, calico, cotton, flannel, gingham, muslin, satin, silk, velvet, velveteen, and wool. Within a quilt, similar types of fabrics should be used, both for ease of handling while making the quilt and for ease of care after it is done. Using unusual fabrics to create special designs is best left to a future quilt, not your first one.

In planning a quilt, fabric color is as important a consideration as texture. This is an area where your own ideas have the greatest influence in determining the personal statement made by the quilt. Some quilters begin planning their project keeping in mind the room where it will be used. Other quilters don't have a set idea of where or how the quilt will eventually be used, but work out their pattern, fabric, and color scheme either to accommodate scraps on hand or out of sheer whimsy. The most important consideration is your own color preferences or the preferences of the person who will eventually be using the quilt.

If the choice of colors or color combinations seems difficult, a color wheel is a helpful tool in planning arrangements. Colored pencils or crayons can be used to plot out color combinations and layouts, and it is a good idea to prepare on paper a sample block in the color arrangement, before finalizing the quilt plan and purchasing the fabric.

The Necessary Tools

Selecting the best possible equipment is an important part of quilting. Accuracy is essential, and proper tools can help ensure accuracy. Here is a list of some of the necessary equipment for a beginning quilter.

A sturdy metal ruler. A ruler is needed for tracing and making patterns. In addition, a good tape measure and a yardstick are also valuable for taking precise measurements; a transparent plastic ruler with grid lines is another handy tool.

Pencils. Colored pencils, as mentioned above, are an excellent way to experiment with different color schemes. Number 2 pencils are useful for tracing templates, outlining designs, tracing quilting patterns, and making other notations.

Graph paper. This is essential for establishing accuracy in designs, as well as for working out new designs.

Tracing paper. This is a helpful tool for copying patterns and making corrections.

Cardboard, plastic, or sandpaper. These are the raw materials needed for making templates or patterns. Cardboard is a favorite for this step of quiltmaking, but sandpaper is also very popular because it grips the fabric and keeps it from slipping as it is being cut. Because both cardboard and sandpaper will deteriorate from use, causing the templates to gradually lose their accuracy, plastic (which can be cut from used containers found around most homes or from plastic sheeting) has become popular. Plastic will not lose its shape and is flexible, transparent, and inexpensive.

Sharp scissors, fine dressmaker's pins, and a good variety and quality of sewing and quilting needles. For cutting and sewing as well as quilting, it is advisable to invest in the best scissors, needles, and pins available. The better these pieces of equipment are, the easier the job will be—both the fabric and the quilter's fingers will be in better condition when the project is completed. It's a good idea to designate one good pair of scissors for cutting cloth only since cutting paper, thread, et cetera will dull them.

Thimbles. Good thimbles also make life easier on the quilter's fingers. Some quilters use two thimbles, one above and one below the fabric, but whatever method is used, nothing will substitute for the best quality tool.

Paper. A handy item is a roll of plain butcher's paper or shelving paper for laying out long quilting motifs or for designing the entire quilt. The same work can be done on sheets of paper taped together, but a continuous roll of paper will make the job easier.

Wax. Paraffin, beeswax, or a candle can be used to strengthen thread, making it slick and easy to pull through fabric.

A quilting frame or hoop. To keep fabric taut during quilting, to ensure smooth, even stitches with no gathers or puckers, a quilting frame is indispensable. A large quilting frame allows one to tackle sizeable areas, while the smaller hoops offer convenience and portability.

An iron and ironing board. Seams that are well pressed as one is working on the quilt will ensure a finished professional look. A pressing cloth is also a good investment as it protects fabrics and gives a crisper finish.

Sewing and quilting thread. Depending on the effect desired, quilting thread may match or contrast with the fabric used in piecing the top. However, the thread should be of an appropriate weight, and its fiber content should be the same as that of the fabric used.

Batting. Again the choice is dependent upon the quilt. Most quilters today prefer the Dacron batts because they are available in many weights, can be either quilted or tied, are completely washable, and can stand up to a great deal of wear. Dacron can give a puffy, thick look to a quilt, or it can easily take a great deal of quilting and give a finer, flatter look to the piece. Some dacron batts are now being made with interlocking fibers to prevent shifting and lumping. But there are some quilters who prefer working with the traditional cotton batting especially when quilting a very traditional design. There are even those quilters who have used wool as batting. Whatever the choice, the quilter should be aware, before purchasing the batting, of the advantages and disadvantages of using that material in a particular quilt.

Backing. Inexpensive unbleached muslin, cotton, flannel, or any of the materials mentioned for use in piecing makes a good choice for the reverse side of the quilt. Your decision should be based on suitability to the quilt, ease of care, and cost. If the quilt is not to be a reversible one, a good muslin is a fine choice, because it is less expensive than a printed or colored cotton fabric.

Trimming. Binding is often used to join the three layers of the quilt. Some quilters make their own bias binding from scraps of the fabric used in the quilt top, while others purchase binding. Either method is acceptable, or alternatively, the quilt can be finished by folding several inches of backing over the top and then blind-stitching.

A sewing machine. This is an optional piece of equipment since there are many quilters who never use a sewing machine for any part of their quilts. Others machine stitch their blocks and piecing and hand quilt. Yet others quilt by machine; several books have been written on machine-stitched quilts.

PLANNING THE QUILT

After assembling the tools, the pattern, and the fabric, be sure to wash and press the material before beginning any cutting. This will ensure that the material will not shrink after the quilt is finished, and will show that the material is dye-fast. Another reason to wash all fabric before beginning is to remove any sizing (or finish) on the fabric, since it is more difficult to handle with sizing.

The Size

New quilters are usually advised to start small. A pillow or small decorative wall hanging are both good first projects. However, if a bed-size quilt is to be your first quilted item, the size of the bed should be the first consideration. Measurements of beds vary, but basically the following are the usual mattress sizes:

Crib: 27" × 48"
Twin: 39" × 75"
Double: 54" × 75"
Queen: 60" × 75"
King: 72" x 84"

Other decisions regarding the finished size must also be taken into account. Is the quilt to be floor length or used with a dust ruffle? Whether the quilt is to reach the floor or to be used with a dust ruffle, measure from the edge of the mattress to the desired length and add that measurement to the sides and the foot of the quilt. If you want the quilt to cover the pillows, add another eighteen to twenty inches.

Sizing Patterns

When planning the elements in your design, try to keep the sizes of all units in harmony with one another. Unify these units by connecting them to each other visually—in terms of color, size, and shape of the individual parts.

Patterns for quilted or appliquéd designs are not always the exact size that you will need, and frequently, you may wish to make a change in one or more parts of the design. One method for enlarging or decreasing the size of designs is to trace the pattern onto a sheet of tissue paper marked with a grid pattern of either one-inch or two-inch squares. On another sheet of paper, draw a grid pattern containing the same number of squares as the original grid, making the squares larger or smaller, depending on whether you wish to reduce or enlarge the design. Then transfer the design from each square on the first paper to the corresponding square on the second sheet until the entire design is the desired size. Graph paper may speed this process.

Another method for enlarging a pattern is to take the design to a photocopy service. This method, while convenient, is often imprecise.

Still another method that could be used is to take a slide of the design and project it on a paper-lined wall in the size required. Moving the projector closer to or away from the wall will adjust the size. Then simply trace around the projected image for a scale pattern. Whatever method is used, accuracy is essential. Time and care should be taken to assure precision results.

Enlarging a Quilt Block

Most traditional pieced quilt designs are based on a square divided into four, nine, sixteen, or more equal squares. This makes enlarging a design based on a block a simple matter.

The first step is to decide how many squares the block contains. An easy method is to cut a square of paper and fold it into the proper number of squares. Using a ruler and a pencil, copy the design onto the opened paper square, using the fold marks as a placement guide. Many designs are based on triangles, diamonds, or other geometric shapes, and can also be copied by marking a square of paper accordingly. Graph paper can be useful for this procedure. Draw a square in the desired size on a sheet of graph paper; determine the number of units in the original block, and then divide your graphed square into the same number of units. Use the grid lines to plot the layout of the finished design.

Some designs are based on diamonds, hexagons, or equilateral triangles. They can be easily plotted on isometric graph paper, which has grids made up of horizontal and diagonal intersecting lines that create the angles necessary for plotting such designs.

Making a Scale Drawing

After careful planning of the blocks or appliqué design, the total quilt top should be considered. Blocks can be sewn together, or can be sewn alternately with plain blocks, or strips can be used as the joining element and become part of the overall design. At the same time, a border or borders should be considered and planned. The last step of the planning stage is to make a scale drawing in color, if possible, of the entire quilt top. This invaluable aid will not only act as a miniature model of the finished product; it is also a useful guide as the quilt is being constructed.

Templates

Once the size of a block or design has been determined and drawn to scale, cutting guides, known as

Nora Mercer's delicate variation of a simple nine-patch block, Radiant Star

Mother/daughter team Byrd and Mary Tribble call their version of a thousand triangles Pyramid Power.

templates, are made. For the transferring of patterns to templates, it is important to work on a smooth, hard surface with good lighting. As with the adapting of a pattern, the template should be made as accurately as possible. An error of a fraction of an inch in a template will be multiplied as you use the template to cut several imprecise pieces. Ultimately, the entire quilt will not fit together properly.

If you use cardboard for the templates and many pieces are to be cut from one template, it is a good idea to make duplicates. Then, as the cardboard wears down, it can be replaced before accuracy is sacrificed. Always number or label all templates. When the cutting process is completed, store all of the pieces for one quilt in a labeled envelope or box.

One way to transfer the pattern onto the template material is to cut out the graph paper pattern and glue it to the cardboard; if sandpaper is being used, glue pattern to its smooth side.

Another method for transferring the pattern to a template is to trace the design onto a piece of tracing paper. Tape this tissue pattern over carbon paper and trace onto cardboard. This method will also work if thin plastic sheets are being used to make the templates.

A light box similar to those used by photographers can also be used to trace the pattern. The light box can be purchased from a photographer's supply store, but also can easily be made at home. For more detailed instruction, see references in the Bibliography.

For the actual cutting of the templates once the design has been transferred, use scissors or a sharp mat knife (art knife) or a razor blade. Carefully cut out the patterns from the cardboard, sandpaper, or plastic. After the template has been cut, be sure to label the piece and to mark the grain line of the fabric on it. The grain refers to the direction of threads lengthwise and crosswise of the fabric. When cutting on the grain the pattern is placed on the straight lengthwise grain of the material. An additional help is to note how many pieces are to be cut in specific colors. When cutting geometric shapes, be sure that at least one side is on the grain of the fabric to prevent stretching.

Some templates include seam allowances and others do not. Depending upon whether the quilt is to be hand or machine stitched, the method of adding seam allowances will vary. For a machine-stitched quilt, precision in adding the seams is extremely important. In a hand-stitched quilt, there is more flexibility.

Some quilters prefer to outline the template on the fabric and use that as a sewing guide. Others prefer to use a ruler to mark the addition of the seam and cut the template with a precise allowance. Still other quilters will add and cut the seam allowance freehand.

Seam allowances vary from $\frac{1}{8}''$ to $\frac{5}{8}''$ with the $\frac{1}{4}''$ used most frequently.

Estimating Yardage

Correctly estimating the yardage is best done after the templates have been made. Most fabrics come in widths of thirty-six or forty-five inches, although occasionally narrower or wider widths will be found. Always include the seam allowances when estimating yardage.

One easy method of determining the amount of fabric needed is to measure out one yard of fabric and see how many times the template can be laid across the width. Remember to keep in mind the grain of the fabric. This should be done for each color to be used. If strips and borders are to be included, measure those carefully as well. You should always add just a little extra (maybe a quarter yard) to the final amount estimated. If bias binding is to be made from one of the fabrics, then that should also be figured into the yardage estimate.

The backing fabric can be estimated easily by using the total measurement of the finished quilt and adding seam allowances. The same estimate, without seam allowances, can be used to determine the amount of batting needed. When buying the fabrics and batting, it is wise to purchase threads to be used and any other sewing supplies not already on hand.

Tracing Patterns and Cutting Fabric

To mark fabric for cutting, place the templates on the *wrong* side of the fabric for patchwork and on the *right* side of the fabric for appliqué. Some patchwork shapes, however, are not reversible, but have definite right and wrong sides to them. Therefore, when dealing with non-reversible shapes, place the template wrong side up on the wrong side of the fabric.

Mark the cutting lines with a sharp pencil. Remember to add seam allowances if the templates do not include them, and adhere to the grain line of the material.

Being sure to use a sharp scissors, cut all the fabric pieces needed. (**Note:** As in fine dressmaking and tailoring, it is best to reserve a good, sharp scissors to be used *only* in cutting fabric—never for cutting paper or other items, which can dull the scissors.)

Assembly

After cutting the fabric, lay out the patchwork shapes in the correct pattern. Any mistakes should show up now, and the entire design can be seen.

As with any sewing project, quilters have varied ways of assembling their work. However, here are a few rules to help beginners. Start by joining the smallest pieces together first. Then progress to joining those parts in rows, if possible. Avoid sewing into corners. Press as you go along for a finished, professional look.

Some piecing can be done by machine. But just as some quilters do all or most of their piecing by machine, others refuse to do even one stitch on a machine and insist on sewing everything by hand. That choice is up to you and may depend upon your selected design. If the piecing is to be done by machine, a common stitch is twelve stitches per inch.

After joining rows or smaller pieces, attach the rows until one block has been completed. Repeat the same steps for each block until all have been completed. Then lay out the blocks as they will appear on the finished quilt before stitching them together. Place any strips or borders in place. Then the total effect can be viewed and if necessary adjusted before the final stitching.

Then proceed to stitch blocks (and stripping, if used) together. Now the quilt is ready to have the borders added.

Borders

The border is an essential element in the entire quilt design. It may seem to be secondary, but it can frame the unit and give it a finished look. Or in some cases, if chosen improperly, the border can detract from an otherwise well-made item. Thus, this part of the quilt should be carefully thought out.

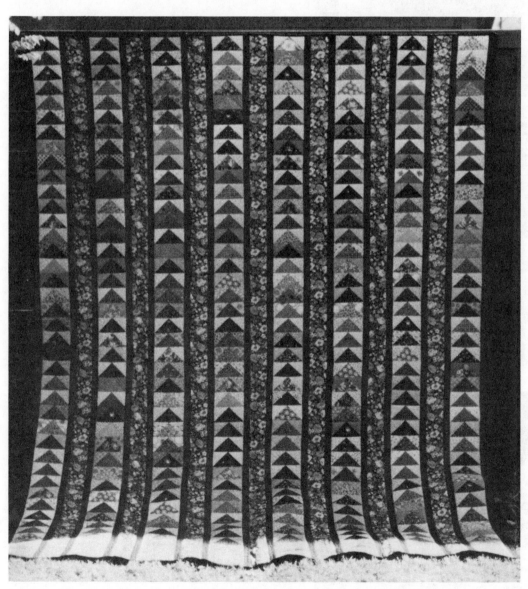

Jacky Dittmer's Flying Geese quilt was pieced in strips

There are three basic methods for joining borders: mitered corners (see figure 1); separate corners (see figure 2); and straight corners (see figure 3).

In the mitered border, the fabric at the corners is cut at a forty-five-degree angle. Two edges joined together at one corner will then form a ninety-degree angle.

For separate corners, a block is added to each corner of the finished cover of the quilt; then the borders are attached to these small blocks.

For a straight finish, two ends of the border will extend across the entire quilt, and the other two borders will fit within the first two.

With the borders attached, the top of the quilt is complete and ready to have the batting and backing added.

Figure 1: Illinois winner Shirley Fomby mitered the outside border of her quilt

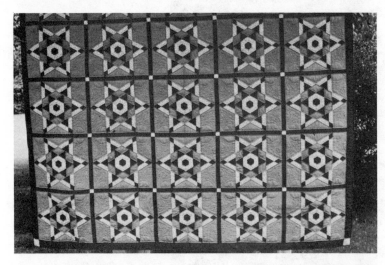

Figure 2: Sandra Tucker's Rising Star quilt features separate corners in both the border and lattice work

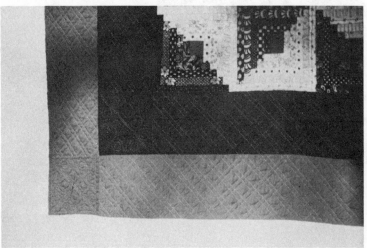

Figure 3: Connecticut's Judi Hoelck finished her quilt with three straight-cornered borders

A striking pieced border accentuates the delicacy of Karen Hagen's skillful appliqué work in Flute, Fronds and Fragrance

Finishing Edges

There are two basic methods for finishing the edges of a quilt. One is to join the three layers—top, batting, and backing—by sewing them together with a binding. This can be a purchased binding or one made from one of the fabrics used in the quilt top.

The other method is to sew together all three layers. In this case the quilt top can be turned onto the back of the quilt and stitched to the backing, or if preferred, the quilt backing can be stitched to the top of the quilt. A third alternative, which is particularly effective if the quilt is to be reversible, is to fold both top and backing fabrics in and slip-stitch them together. This is especially desirable if the pattern itself has detail that lends itself to this finish, for example, a double wedding ring quilt, with scalloped edges.

Wendy Analla's Dresden Plate *quilt features scalloped edges*

31

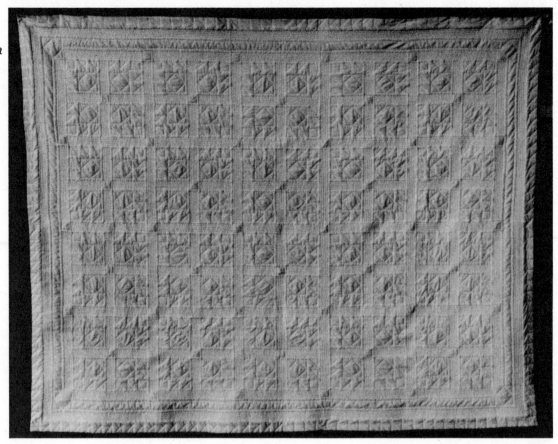

Quilting

Most quilting is done by hand, but some contemporary pieces lend themselves to machine-quilting. Again, this is the decision of the quiltmaker.

If the piece is to be machine-quilted, the layers must be pinned together or very well basted, and it is best to quilt from the center outward.

For hand-quilting, a hoop or a quilting frame should be used. The advantages of a quilt frame are that more than one person can work on the quilt at one time, but, on the other hand, the quilt frame does take up room.

Whichever method is decided upon, you should lay out and mark the quilt pattern before stitching. A particular quilt pattern may lend itself to a particular type of quilting, but for most projects the variations of the quilt designs are almost unlimited. Scrolls, feathers, flowers, straight lines, circles, and representational subjects may be quilted at whatever point you decide is best. One or more designs may be used on the body of the quilt, and a contrasting or varied quilting pattern may be used on borders. Some areas may be heavily quilted and others left with more open areas to achieve a puffier look and feel.

Quilting designs can be transferred onto the top of the quilt with the use of carbon paper. Care should be taken not to smudge the carbon. An art gum eraser is handy for removing tracings or pencil marks after the quilting is completed.

Another method is to use a quilt pattern. Make the pattern, cut it out, place it on the quilt top, and outline it in pencil. Some quilters draw their own designs freehand on the quilt. Whatever the choice, as in the previous procedures, planning will ensure the best results.

To highlight a pattern, it is best never to quilt on a seam line but rather to quilt ¼ to ½ inch inside or outside the seam. When working on a pieced design, it is effective to quilt as many parts of the patch as possible to give it definition. However, it is not necessary to quilt around each piece, or for that matter to quilt around every seam line.

The quilting stitches must be taken through all three layers. Beginners should concentrate on even stitches rather than just small stitches. A goal of eight to ten stitches per inch should be kept in mind. Very thick fabric, however, will necessitate larger stitches, done in an up-and-down working manner, rather than the running stitch, which is more feasible on lighter weight fabrics.

Whether working on a quilt frame, a hoop, or sim-

Starshine & Shadow No. 2 by Carole C. Quam, page 38. (PHOTO BY TOM CRESAP)

Cherokee Trail of Tears by
Chris Wolf Edmonds, page 74.
(PHOTO BY ROY HALE)

Patronage of the Arts by
Shirley Fomby, page 68.
(PHOTO COURTESY OF THE
ARTIST)

*Feathery border motif,
from Donna Andrew's*
Calendulas *(see page 134)*

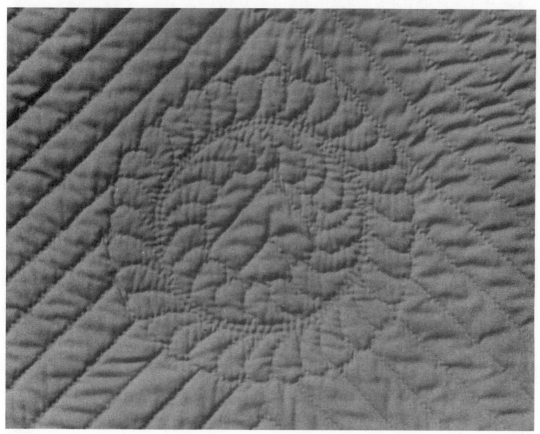

*Detail of Ernestine Costas'
quilt (see page 132)*

ply with the quilt in your lap, it is best to work from the center out. That way, if any puffiness or unevenness appears, it can be remedied more readily. A medium-length thread should be used (seventeen to eighteen inches) to avoid tangling while quilting. Knots should not be visible on the top of the quilt. To finish off an end, double back through the top layer about five or six stitches, just as though you were quilting backward. Then go through the batt and take a long stitch before returning to the surface. Take a small stitch, go through the batt again, bring the needle to the top and clip the thread close to the fabric. The end of the thread will be drawn back into the quilt and will disappear.

Remember that as with most accomplishments, practice and patience are the necessary ingredients. No matter how large your first stitches are, how difficult your first project seems, quilting is a real and lasting achievement.

For those readers who are interested in learning to quilt, there are many fine books available that give much more detailed directions for beginners. And in many communities throughout the country, there are quilting classes available.

A word about the instructions in this book:

It is remarkable how clear and precise so many quilters can be in giving directions for making their favorite quilts. Naturally, they don't use exactly the same terminology, but we have given directions as they have shared them with us. Measurements vary: for example, two quilts labeled "queen size" may have different dimensions. Some quilts are meant to be floor length while others are used to cover just the top and sides of the bed.

Similarly, directions and methods for assembly may differ. The instructions for all quilts are meant to be a guide which the individual quilter may adapt to suit personal tastes.

Chapter 4

THE WINNERS

THOSE WERE THE DAYS

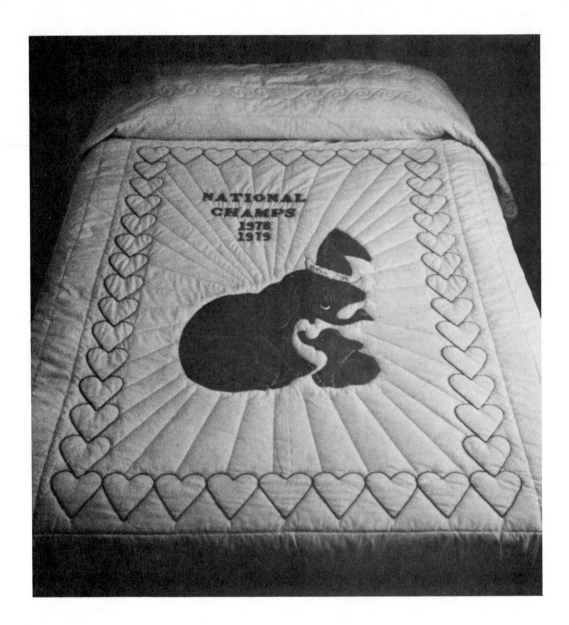

*D*ramatic red appliqué on a simple white background gives this tribute quilt
its special spirit. What better way to commemorate an outstanding
achievement than by making a permanent mememto of it?

Annie Mauch won First Prize at the Dothan National Peanut Festival
in the sewing category for arts and crafts with her quilt, Those Were the
Days. The quilt, which also won Grand Prize in the sewing and clothing
category, was a tribute to the University of Alabama football team, which
had won the national championship.

When Annie picked up her winning quilt at the close of the festival, the women in charge of the displays informed her that the quilt was a "true winner!" The judges, who were real fans of Auburn University, the University of Alabama's rival, couldn't deny the excellence of the workmanship, the appeal of the design, and the quality of the quilting motif.

This quilt was made as a gift to Marcia Hatcher, a graduate of the University of Alabama, now a United States marshall. Marcia's mother, Opal Hatcher, did much of the embroidery and appliqué work. Annie drafted the entire design and did the major part of the hand-quilting and binding.

Annie's maternal grandmother was well known for her quilting ability during the late 1800s and early 1900s in Mansfield, Arkansas. But it was from observing her paternal grandmother, who lived with the family, that Annie gained her first-hand knowledge of quilting.

Her advice to beginning quilters is "Practice, patience, and don't give up. **Do it!** *The journey begins with a positive attitude. A winner is anyone who at least tries. Do not let the 'I can't' thought defeat you. Experiment with small projects for patchwork and piecing and easy-to-follow fabric designs to learn the actual quilting process."*

Using the University of Alabama's school colors of red and white, Those Were the Days *shows the school's mascot, the elephant. The two elephants might represent a father and son reliving the grand times of the championship Crimson Tide Team. Perhaps he had played during the years the team was National Champion.*

The elephant designs are framed with a heart pattern; the outline of the heart is embroidered with red floss. Outside of the hearts, the quilting motif is done in a curved wave pattern. The entire quilting design was traced onto a queen-size sheet and hand quilted. The back and border are red cotton-polyester fabric.

STARSHINE & SHADOW NO. 2

*T*his boldly patterned, vividly colored quilt borrows from Amish quilts the brilliant interaction of deep and warm hues, and boasts the added richness of luxurious fabrics such as satin and intensely colored cottons. The strong central figure and background design are echoed in the geometric precision of the quilting, both in the border and in the overall quilt design.

Carole Quam came away from the Alaska State Fair quilt competition in 1982 with three top awards for her quilt Starshine & Shadow. She won Best of Show (Stearns & Foster), Grand Prize for quilting, and First Place in the whole or partly machine-made division.

Carole has been quilting only since 1976 and just began hand-quilting three years ago. She is a self-taught quilter who advises beginners, "Don't be afraid to experiment. Do what feels right to you in pattern, colors, materials, quilting. Don't rush a project." She works with cottons, blends, washable satins, and velveteens. This original design was Carole's first entry in a quilt competition. It is the second in a series she has been working on. Carole greatly admires Amish quilts and has been experimenting with creating greater color intensity and depth through the juxtaposition of similar shades.

"While I was laying the pieces out on the floor for my first quilt to study the color effect, my son took one look at it and said, 'Gee, that's sure going to be an ugly quilt, Mom.' That first quilt then became 'Little Ugly.' This second quilt is a bit larger, and so is known as 'Big Ugly.'"

MATERIALS

Rich-looking and rich-feeling fabrics, such as satins, velvets, and cottons, in the blue (deep green, plum, navy, and purple) and red (gold, orange) families.

CUTTING GUIDE

Templates include ¼″ seam allowance.

Color A: solid purple cotton
  Figure 1–1
  Figure 2–4
  Figure 3–4

Color B: solid plum cotton
  Figure 1–4
  Figure 2–16
  Figure 3–16

Color C: emerald green satin
  Figure 1–4
  Figure 2–8

Color D: assorted gold and golden orange cottons
  Figure 1–48
  Figure 2–12
  Figure 3–24

Color E: assorted medium shades of blues and greens in cotton and satin
  Figure 1–136
  Figure 3–32

Color F: assorted deep shades of blues, greens, and purples in cotton
  Figure 1–36
  Figure 3–24

Color G: darkest navy cotton for border

Color H: medium blue cotton for border

Color I: purple cotton binding

ASSEMBLY

The quilt may be pieced by hand or machine. Dimensions of the finished quilt depend on the size of the individual module selected; using a 2″ square (figure 1) will yield a finished quilt measuring 54″ × 54″, including borders. Using a 2½″ square will make a quilt 67.5″ × 67.5″, and a 3″ square will make a quilt 81″ × 81″.

Because *Starshine & Shadow No. 2* is an overall design, and not composed of blocks, the pieces may be assembled in any order or method preferred by the maker. It is advisable, however, to arrange all cut pieces of the central figure on a flat surface before joining, to assure a pleasing and effective placement of colors.

After completing piecing of central figure, attach 1″ border in darkest navy cotton. Surrounding this, attach a 3″ border in medium blue cotton. (For both borders, add ¼″ seam allowance when cutting.) The quilt is finished with a narrow binding in purple cotton.

The finished quilt is then quilted by machine or hand as shown in the Quilting Design.

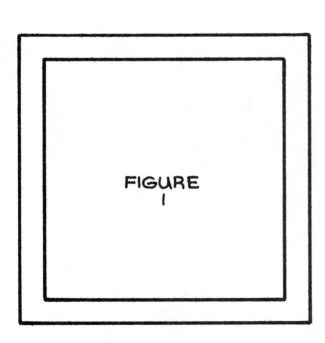

FIGURE 1

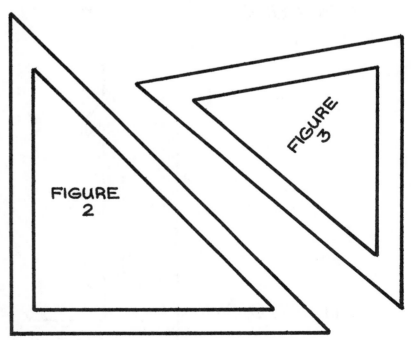

FIGURE 2

FIGURE 3

PIECING GUIDE

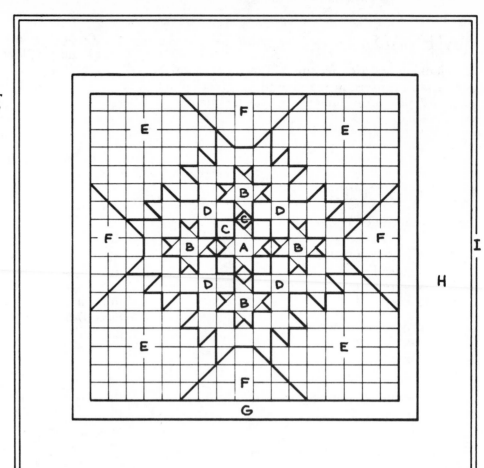

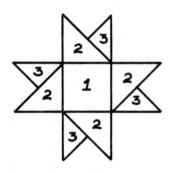

SMALL STAR
PIECING GUIDE

QUILTING DESIGN

40

VIRGINIA "GINGER" THOMPSON · *Kingman, Arizona*

AUTUMN LEAVES

*T*he harvest of fall is gracefully depicted in this quilt. Variation in background fabric gives Autumn Leaves *added dimension.*

Mrs. Thompson began her Autumn Leaves *(Light and Shadow) quilt while the family was living in Alaska. "I did it during the dark days to fend off cabin fever—I succeeded." This was her first entry into competition and it has won three prizes: First Prize at the Mohave County Fair; First Prize in the Arizona State Fair for appliquéd quilts; and Best Appliquéd Quilt at the Arizona Quilters Guild.*

"There were many times in the three years (on and off) of working on the quilt that I thought I had taken on too much. Using the county fair as a goal helped give the push I needed to finish." Ginger was fortunate to have had a grandmother who quilted and remembers watching her quilt. Ginger's advice to beginners is, "Start small with manageable projects. I like a lap frame for maneuverability, but have used both the big frame and lap."

Currently, Ginger is working on a group quilt with nine friends. She also has a pieced Bear Paw and a Yo-Yo quilt in progress.

QUILTING DESIGN

MATERIALS

Fabric for leaves in fall colors, small print, either 100 percent cotton or 65 percent cotton/35 percent polyester. Background fabric should be a neutral color, either three shades for a light and shadow effect or just one color.

CUTTING GUIDE

Cut 72 blocks, 8½" square (which allows for ¼" seam allowance) from solid color fabric:

    20 beige (1 yard)
    28 light brown (1½ yards)
    24 gray (1½ yards)
            or
    4 yards of one color

Draw leaf design (figure 1) on back of printed fabric for 72 leaves.

Stay-stitch around each leaf, cut out leaves adding sufficient fabric for seam allowance.

ASSEMBLY

Autumn Leaves may be pieced and quilted by hand or machine. It includes appliqué and embroidery.

PIECING GUIDE

(L—Light brown, B—Beige, G—Grey)

L	B	L	L	L	L	B	L
B	B	L	L	L	L	L	B
L	G	G	G	G	G	G	L
L	G	G	B	B	G	G	L
B	G	G	B	B	G	G	B
L	G	G	B	B	G	G	L
L	G	G	G	G	G	G	L
B	B	L	L	L	L	B	B
L	B	L	L	L	L	B	L

Clip curves of leaves to angles. Press seam allowance under and baste, or use small pieces of double-faced fusible interfacing while ironing.

Pin each leaf diagonally to a square and appliqué in place. Embroider stem (carrying out into block) and veins on each block, using outline stitch. Arrange blocks, 8 across and 9 down, with leaves at various angles. See chart opposite for block color placement. This will provide a quilt top that is 64" × 72".

Four 4½" border strips (this allows for ¼" seam allowance) in small prints to complement the leaf colors were added to provide a quilt top to fit a queen-size bed with a dust ruffle. The backing consists of a 6-yard piece of light-colored calico cut in half and sewn lengthwise. Back, batting, and top are basted together securely, so that the cover is ready to be quilted.

This quilt was worked entirely on a lap frame, quilting from the center out. For a trapunto effect inside each square, quilt three times around each leaf, as shown in Quilting Design.

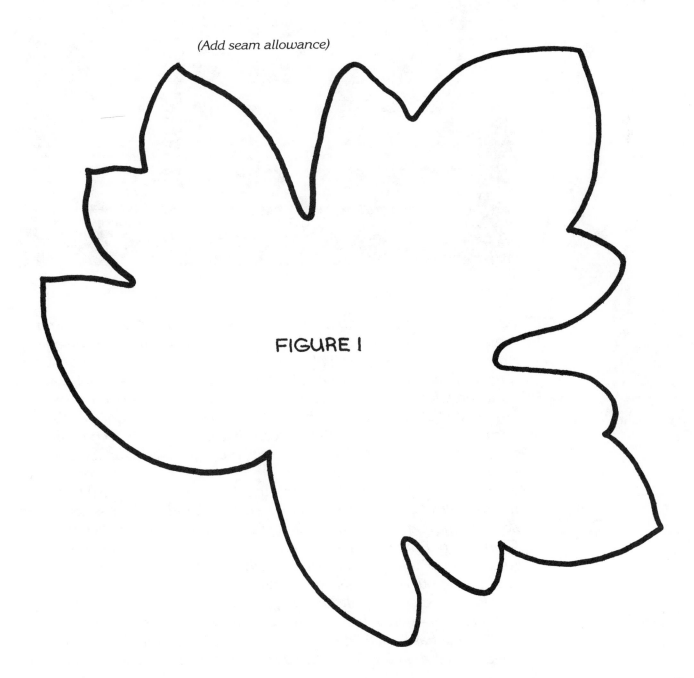

(Add seam allowance)

FIGURE I

43

BEAR PAW

*T*he crisp simplicity of the blue sprigged fabric and the white contrasting material combine to show this Bear Paw design to beautiful advantage. Adding the intricate hand-quilting to this fine example of a classic creates a result similar to a reversible quilt; the back of this piece resembles a white-on-white quilt, while the top is a dramatic example of pure design.

When Patricia Eaton and her family moved to New Mexico in 1978 because of her husband's job transfer, she found herself in a community where she knew no one. To keep herself busy, she signed up for a quilt class.

"The day of the first class came, and I was nervous. It wasn't five minutes after that class started that we were relaxed, and I was completely sold on learning to quilt." Eventually Patricia became a member of the Grant County Quilters Guild. "We had no officers, no dues, and no real rules. We met twice a month in each other's homes and had a great time working on our own quilts and sharing patterns, tips, and that 'quilt talk' that is so much fun. I called it therapy because if you went to a meeting feeling awful—you always came out feeling great."

Patricia has won First Place in the hand-pieced and hand-quilted category at the Boone County Extension Homemakers Annual Quilt Show *with her* Bear Paw. *Her advice to beginning quilters is: "First, don't be in a hurry. Second, don't give up. Third, read everything you can find. Fourth, strive for neatness, accuracy, and nice color combinations. And even if you are using a purchased pattern, put something in it that is your own idea. And finally, take a class if one is available."*

MATERIALS

Printed or plain colored fabric in a deep shade and a contrasting material in white or a lighter color for the background.

CUTTING GUIDE

All measurements and templates do *not* include seam allowances.

    Color A: printed or colored fabric
        Figure 1–100
        Figure 2–320
                168 (for borders)
        Figure 4–80

    Color B: white or light-colored plain fabric
        Figure 1–80
        Figure 2–320
                168 (for borders)
        Figure 3–80
        Figure 5–80

ASSEMBLY

Bear Paw is hand- or machine-pieced and hand-quilted. Each square is 16″. There are 20 squares in the quilt. These are surrounded by a white 2¼″ lattice with a 2¼″ square of print fabric at each corner. Surrounding the squares and lattice is a print border 2¼″ wide. Around that border is a white border 2¼″ wide. The final border is done in blue and white triangles.

To piece squares, join together one bear claw as illustrated in piecing guide. For a complete block, assemble 4 bear paws and arrange them so they are pointed outward. Join claws with border strips and one small square (figure 1). Repeat for all 20 blocks, joining them with lattice strips and small squares as shown in the Piecing Guide.

To finish the quilt top, attach a 2¼″ border in the print fabric, followed by another 2¼″ border in white. Finally, piece the print/white sawtooth border and attach. Bind the quilt top, batting, and backing with binding made from the printed material.

The large square of each paw is quilted ¼″ inside

QUILTING DESIGN

PIECING GUIDE

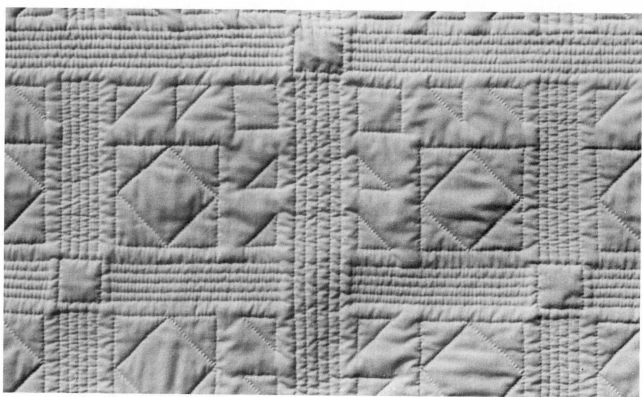

A detail of the back of Bear Paw, *shown in full on page 26.*

the square and then a square within the square (see Quilting Design). The small corner squares are quilted ¼″ inside and the small white squares and triangles are all quilted ¼″ inside each one. The strips between each of the paws are quilted in straight lines ¼″ apart, and so is the lattice work and the white border. The blue border is quilted ¼″ inside each seam.

The quilt is bound in bias binding made from the same printed fabric, to form a quilt approximately 91″ × 111″.

Template Figures do not include seam allowance

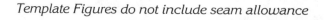

FIGURE 4

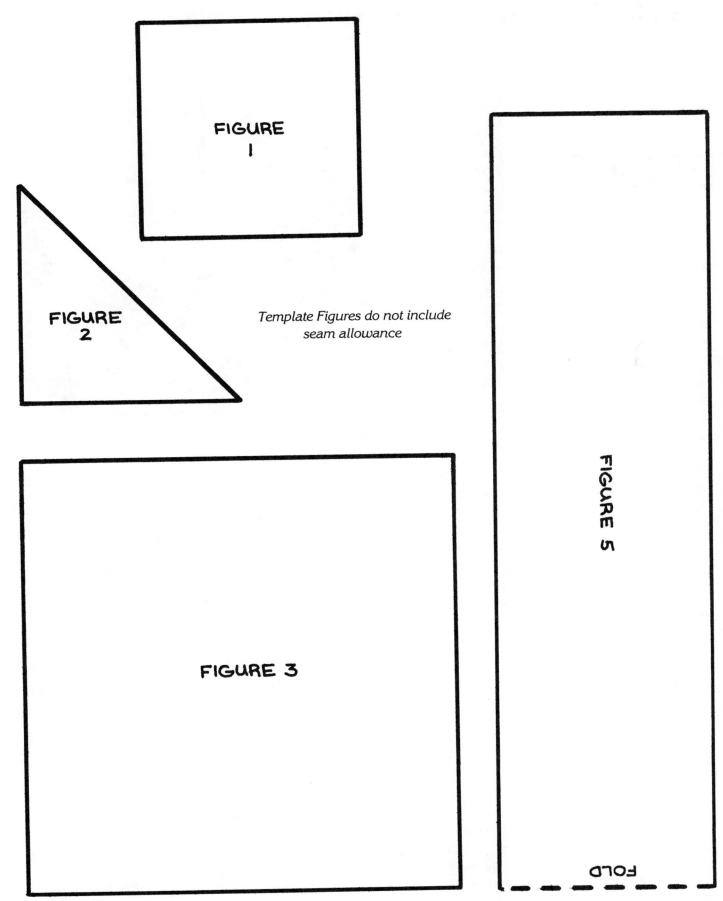

FIGURE
1

FIGURE
2

FIGURE 3

Template Figures do not include
seam allowance

FIGURE 5

FOLD

BROKEN STAR

*I*n this example of the Broken Star pattern, the interaction of the solid components and the colorful areas combine to produce a three-dimensional work that appeals to the touch as well as the eye. The rich variety of shapes and quilting result in a work that continually gives its viewer something new to discover.

Shirley McGavren's quilt, Broken Star, won First Prize and Best of Class at the Marin Quilt and Needlecraft Show in 1981 and First Prize at the Santa Clara County Fair in 1982. The Marin show was her first judged show.

She was first introduced to quilting as a child during the Depression when her mother's weekly sewing group started making quilts. Today her lovely creations have prompted her daughter and daughter-in-law to begin quilting.

Shirley pursued her quilting and with each quilt her technique improved. When she saw a copy of The Quilters, by Patricia Cooper and Norma Bradley Buferd, she says, "It was love at first sight with the beautiful old Broken Star shown on the cover. After reading an article about the story behind Broken Star, I knew I had to try and reproduce this quilt for myself. Whoever made the original was truly an artist in her use of color and pattern, and the quilting appears to be magnificent. Making this quilt proved to be quite a challenge because, with star patterns, everything must be perfection as you proceed or the end result will be a rippled mess instead of a beautiful flat quilt top. I learned patience and the importance *of complete accuracy with seam allowances, et cetera, as I ripped many a faulty seam."*

Her advice to beginners: "Go to as many quilt shows and displays as possible. Study the workmanship, especially the very old quilts."

MATERIALS

100% cotton fabrics in colors listed in Cutting Guide or any combination that quilter desires. Scraps, remnants or yardage may be used. Cotton backing and polyester batting.

CUTTING GUIDE

Using pattern shown in figure 1 (seam allowance *not* included) cut diamond-shaped patches, using the following color code:

A–red (solid)	184
B–light yellow (print)	112
C–beige (print)	192
D–pink (print)	32
E–black (print)	160
F–olive green (solid)	168
G–gray (print)	40
H–red (print)	72
I–bright yellow (print)	72
J–multicolored print on white background	120
Total	1152 patches

Note: Diamond patches must always be cut with two sides of the patch on the straight of the fabric.

ASSEMBLY

Joining Diamond Patches:

Center star of quilt is made up of 8 identical pieced diamond-shaped sections meeting at center point; each section is made up of 6 rows of 6 diamond patches each. See figure 2 for 1 section.

The outer portion of the large star is made up of 24 more diamond-shaped sections joined for a circular design. See figure 3 for these sections.

Proceed to make 32 diamond-shaped sections as follows:

Make 8 sections using figure 2.
Make 24 sections using figure 3.

To make each section, stitch together 6 rows as shown in figures 2 and 3. When joining diamonds to

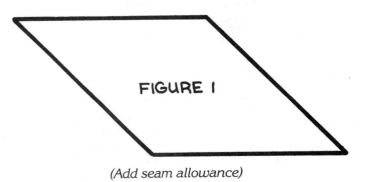

FIGURE I

(Add seam allowance)

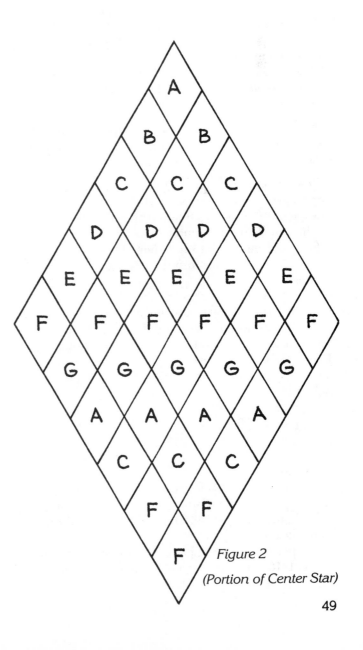

Figure 2

(Portion of Center Star)

form a row, stitch patches together along sides cut on straight of goods, stitching from wide-angled corner toward the pointed ends. Trim seams at points as you piece. Matching corners carefully, join the 6 rows together to make a diamond-shaped section. (When joining rows, you will be stitching along bias edges, so keep thread taut enough to prevent stretching of material.) Press seams of each section to one side.

Assembling Sections:

For center star, join 4 sections for each half, then join both halves. Each point of star should measure 12″ (plus outside seam allowance) along side edges.

For background blocks, cut a pattern 12″ square. Mark 16 blocks on wrong side of background fabric, such as unbleached muslin, and add ¼″ seam allowance all around. Cut out squares.

For background triangles, cut square pattern in half diagonally to form triangle pattern. Cut 8 triangles from the same background fabric, again adding ¼″ seam allowance.

Sew 8 square background blocks to center star, fitting two sides of the block between two points of the star.

Note: From here on, it is important to press frequently and to be certain that the work continues to lie flat as each section is added.

Sew remaining diamond-shaped sections (pieced per figure 3) into 8 groups of 3 sections each, and sew each 3-pointed section in the wide angle formed by the square background blocks.

Sew adjacent sections together.

Sew the 8 triangles into the open spaces along the 4 sides.

Corner Squares:

Each corner square contains a small star made up of 8 sections, and each section is made up of 2 rows. See figures 4 and 5. Make 2 small stars using figure 4, and 2 small stars using figure 5. These four small stars will require cutting 128 diamond patches as follows:

    Color B—16
    Color C—16
    Color D—16
    Color G—16
    Color H—64

For background blocks for the corner squares, make a pattern of a 4″ square. Transfer to wrong side of background fabric and mark 16 blocks, adding ¼″ seam allowance all around.

Cut pattern in half diagonally for triangle pattern and cut 16 triangles, again adding ¼″ seam allowance.

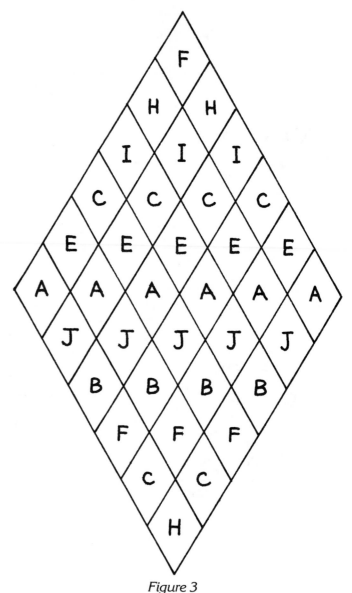

Figure 3
(Portion of Outer Star)

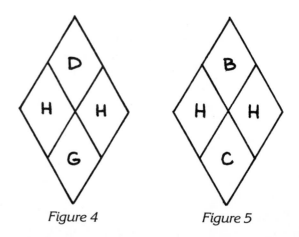

Figure 4   Figure 5

50

Assemble corner squares and insert into 4 corners of quilt top.

To form border, use pattern for triangle used in the 4 corner squares. Cut 92 triangles from background material used in quilt and 92 triangles from a desired print or solid color. Sew together into squares and into strips, forming a sawtooth pattern.

Add strips to four sides of quilt. Bind quilt with bias binding.

Quilt, using the Quilting Design on all the background blocks. Additional quilting can be added according to the quilter's preference.

All the other quilting follows the lines of the piecing.

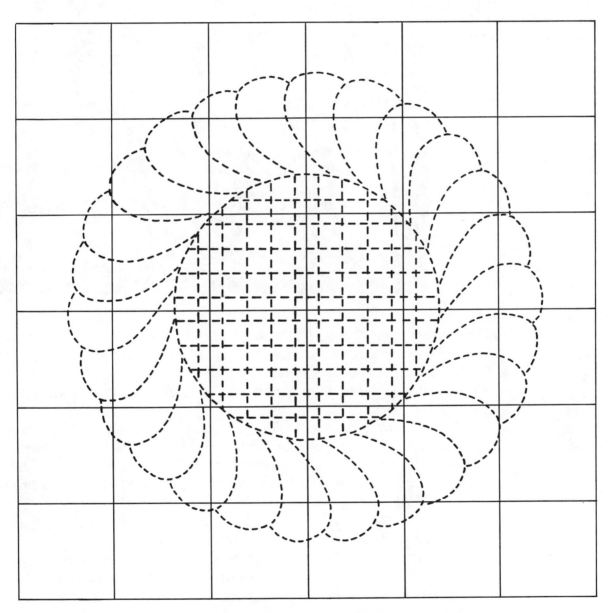

QUILTING DESIGN
(shown at 50 percent of full size; use the graph lines to enlarge to full size)

SUE BOSLEY · *Lamar, Colorado*

DOUBLE WEDDING RING

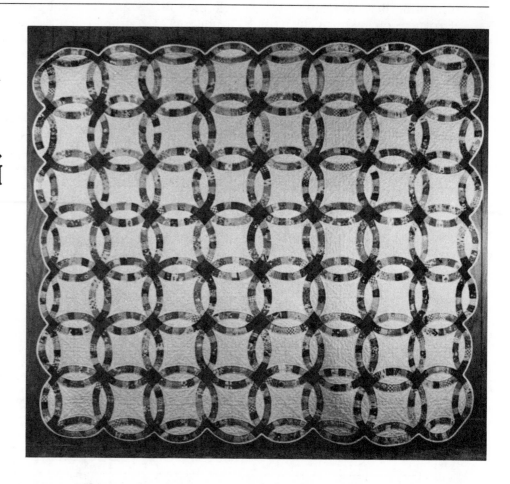

*T*his excellent version of the Double Wedding Ring pattern is especially appealing because of the choice of a simple white background with the multicolored rings. The rhythm of the circles is enhanced by Sue's personal touch of quilting, an adaptation of the fleur-de-lis that is part of the Bosley family coat of arms.

Sue Bosley's Double Wedding Ring won First Place in the all-hand-work category of the Colorado State Fair. She learned quilting from books and by asking questions of experienced quilters. She is the first in her family to quilt. "My mother raised a large family and most of her time was spent patching. Her patching was a work of art!"

Though many quilters tell of the support of their projects by their husbands and families, Sue's story is a little special.

"I was away at a meeting in Denver. A tornado watch was in effect for our area. My husband wrapped our quilt in plastic and placed it where he could easily pick it up on his way out of the house so that it would be safe.

"My husband was the driving force in my completion of our quilt. He encouraged me, praised me and cried with me when we saw the First Place ribbon at the Colorado State Fair."

This is Sue's first quilt.

MATERIALS

7 yards assorted prints
1½ yards of solid or deep color to set segments together
5½ yards white fabric

CUTTING GUIDE

Templates include ¼″ seam allowance.

Figure 1–56 center pieces (**Note:** Fabric is folded *twice* and template must be placed on 2 fold lines.)

Figure 2–280 pieces: 140 in navy and 140 in navy with white polka dots

Figure 3–508 pieces in assorted prints (half are cut in reverse in order to continue the contour of the circle).

Figure 4–1,016 pieces in assorted prints

Figure 5–127 pieces in white, placed on fold.

ASSEMBLY

Join 4 pieces cut from figure 4. On each end of this section, join 1 piece cut from figure 3. Remember, 1 of the 2 pieces cut from figure 3 must be reversed to complete the contour of the circle. These 6 pieces complete 1 segment of the wedding band.

Fit a segment to each side of a center cut from figure 5, and join. It is best to pin the segments and center pieces together at ends and center, allowing any fullness to be worked in gradually.

Sew 1 piece cut from figure 2 to each end of segments, to complete 1 melon-shaped piece. Remember, 1 end piece should be navy and the other should be navy with white polka dots. By piecing all 127 melon-shaped pieces before beginning to set your quilt together, you will have a better picture of what the overall quilt will look like. This will allow you to rearrange blocks to make the quilt more attractive.

Now sew a melon-shaped piece to each of the 4 sides of the wedding-band center to make a complete circle. To one side of this circle sew another wedding-band center to which only 3 melon-shaped pieces have been added. Continue adding portions of blocks as needed.

Quilt may be finished off with scalloped edges or bound straight.

Quilt the melon-shaped and center pieces using the Quilting Designs.

The finished quilt measures 85″ × 99″.

PIECING GUIDE

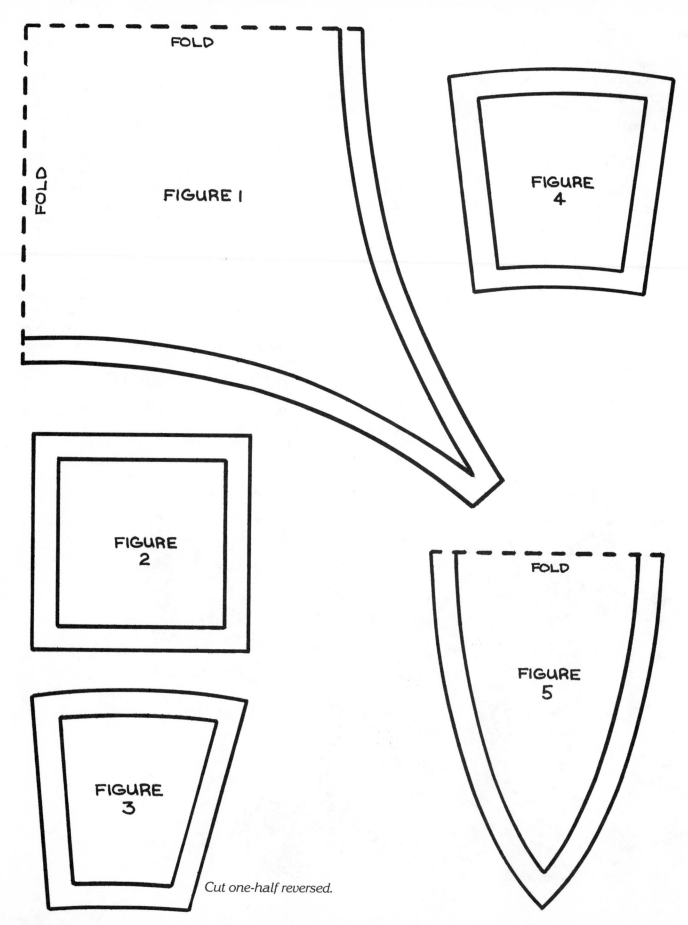

FOLD

FOLD

FIGURE 1

FIGURE 4

FIGURE 2

FIGURE 3

Cut one-half reversed.

FOLD

FIGURE 5

54

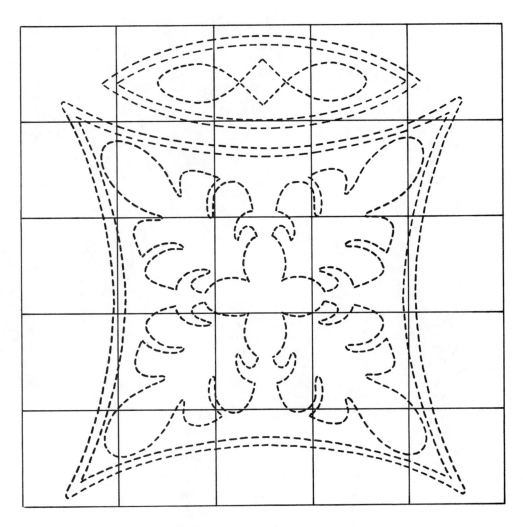

QUILTING DESIGNS

(shown at 50 percent of full size; use the graph lines to enlarge to full size)

JUDI HOELCK · *Wallingford, Connecticut*

LOG CABIN

*T*hough the Log Cabin pattern was one of the earliest quilt designs, this striking example has a contemporary look. The immediate effect is one of simplicity, but this is misleading because many well-conceived details of design, color placement, and borders have meshed to produce this brilliant quilt.

Made entirely by hand, **Log Cabin** has already taken seven top prizes across the country. Judi Hoelck is a self-taught quilter who began entering quilt competitions in 1979. No one else in her family quilts and Judi has been quilting only for about six years.

"Making a quilt is a purely relaxing and enjoyable pastime. I enjoy it so much, I never use a sewing machine. Hand-piecing also helps me practice small stitching for the quilting part."

Log Cabin is her favorite pattern. "I like a pattern where you can use very small pieces. Log Cabin is also variable. You can take this most traditional pattern and make it uniquely your own."

MATERIALS

An equal amount of light and dark fabric. Early Log Cabin quilts were made of wool, later they were made of silk, and today cotton or cotton-polyester is used equally successfully.

CUTTING GUIDE

The cutting guide is for each block; there are 100 blocks in the quilt. Templates do *not* include seam allowance.

Color A: assorted dark printed fabrics cut, 1 for each figure 2 through 10.

Color B: assorted light printed fabrics cut, 1 each for figures 3 through 12.

Color C: a medium-colored fabric to join together the light and dark strips cut, figure 1-1

To ensure alignment when using striped or patterned fabrics, place templates carefully on wrong side of fabric and mark before cutting.

ASSEMBLY

To piece blocks, begin with a square segment (figure 1) and join the shortest strip (figure 2) to one side. Attach the next longest strip (figure 3) in the darker fabric to these 2 and continue to add strips in a counterclockwise direction, alternating dark and light fabrics. Repeat for all 100 blocks.

The completed blocks are joined in strips, which are then sewed together to form the quilt top. One of the unique aspects of the Log Cabin quilt is the many variations that can be achieved simply by rearranging the finished quilt blocks. Here the orientation of the blocks is alternated to create a pinwheel effect, but the possibilities for new arrangements are nearly endless.

To finish the quilt, attach three 4½″ borders (add ¼″ seam allowance when cutting) and join the quilt top, batting, and backing without a binding.

To quilt, stitch each block ¼″ inside the seam line, starting inside the central square and spiraling outward counterclockwise with one continuous line of stitching. The central squares and borders can be quilted in floral or geometric designs of the quilter's choosing. The borders on this quilt are diagonally crosshatched at 1″ intervals in an interesting herringbone pattern—2 close-set parallel lines intersected by a single line of stitching.

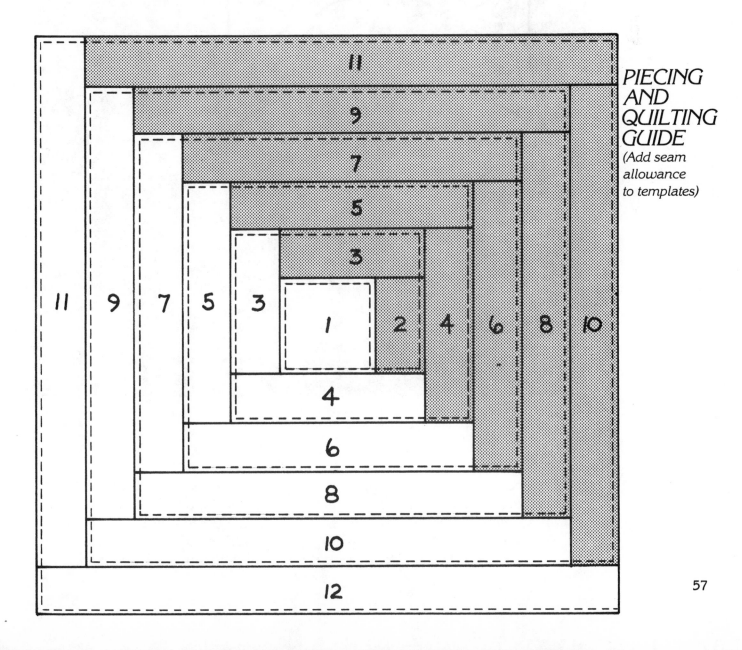

*PIECING
AND
QUILTING
GUIDE*
(Add seam
allowance
to templates)

RIBBON QUILT

*I*ngenuity combined with years of skillful needlework have produced this prizewinning quilt, which makes clever use of prizewinning ribbons. The placement of the ribbons makes for a pleasing overall effect, and the luster of the fabrics adds an unusual dimension to this quilt.

Last year Mary Jester won thirty-eight blue ribbons and twenty-seven red ribbons at the Delaware State Fair in the Needlework Division competitions. She and her husband live and work on the 225-acre farm where Mr. Jester was born. In addition, Mary is a hairdresser.

"I go from 6:00 A.M. to 10:00 P.M. every day, and when I sit down for a few minutes it's just natural for me to pick up a piece of my handwork." Every morning Mary gets up to make her husband's breakfast, and while she waits for him to finish the milking she does some of her prizewinning quilting or needlework. She is seventy-six years old and plans to keep working.

Mary's one word of advice to beginning quilters is "Patience." She uses any and all kinds of fabric for her quilts and both cotton and polyester batting—whatever is available.

At last count she had over seven hundred ribbons, and the only sad note is that she wasn't able to fit them all onto this ribbon quilt.

In fact there are 169 ribbons on this appliquéd quilt, which Mary Jester designed in order "to do something with all those ribbons."

The ribbons are appliquéd on the quilt top with machine-stitching. The top is then quilted to the batting and backing, following the design of the ribbons. Additional quilting designs are added between the ribbons. A blue binding is added to complete the quilt.

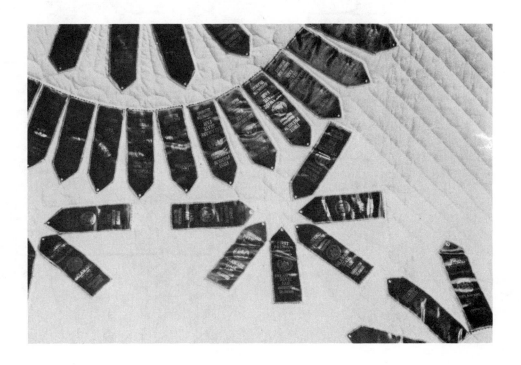

DIXIE HAYWOOD · *Pensacola, Florida*

VICTORIANA

A dazzling adaptation of the crazy quilt, the earliest form of patchwork quilting, has resulted in this opulent free-form design. The deep, rich fabrics
and colors pay fitting tribute to the fanciful Victorian era.
Victoriana *was awarded First Place for "Innovative Use of a Traditional*

Design," at the Minnesota Quilters Winter Fantasy, a quilt conference held in Minneapolis featuring quilts from around the nation. It was again awarded First Place (in fiber) at the Great Gulf Coast Art Festival in Pensacola.

"I named the quilt Victoriana because it is the closest to the Victorian crazy quilt style that inspired my work. My contemporary crazy-quilt method is different both in technique and intent from Victorian work, and the name is meant to be a somewhat humorous indication of my philosophy that we honor and acknowledge the past best by building on it, not repeating it." She has entered her quilts in judged shows for about five years.

Dixie's advice to beginning quilters is, "Don't bite off more than you can chew. There are many simple patterns that make smashing quilts. Choose a pattern that you can enjoy working with at the skill level you have. Then you'll be pleased with the result and will be encouraged to increase your range and repertoire."

Dixie, who is a self-taught quilter and the author of two books on quilting, credits the quilt's completion to her husband's assistance. "He cooked and cleaned so that I would have the time to work on it without distraction."

The pattern was inspired by the design possibilities inherent in the log cabin type of quilt. Each block is divided diagonally into light and dark areas, and the resulting overall design is determined by the arrangement of the blocks.

In the case of Victoriana, rather than using the strips (or "logs") of the log cabin pattern, she divided the block diagonally into a solid velveteen area and a crazy-quilted area. Except for four crazy-quilted squares and the border, the entire quilt is done with squares formed from a crazy-quilted triangle and a velveteen triangle.

Victoriana uses both cotton velveteen and cotton calico and is embellished with stitchery done in velvet thread. It is one hundred inches square; the design of the front is repeated in wine and burgundy cotton on the back.

This quilt is finished in an octagonal shape, and is edged with a binding made from the same burgundy fabric.

ELIZABETH H. GARRISON · *Statesboro, Georgia*

LONE STAR

While the Lone Star design is frequently seen at quilt shows, this finely executed example uses an unusual color combination against the solid background. The geometric design of the quilt is offset by intricate feather quilting on the border.

Dr. Elizabeth Garrison is a retired professor who taught Science for Elementary Teachers at Georgia Southern College. Her **Lone Star** (also frequently referred to as **Texas Star**) has won four First Prizes at shows throughout Georgia, including the Statesboro Regional Arts and Crafts Show and the Quilt Georgia Show, 1983.

Dr. Garrison's quilt workbasket has accompanied her on a freighter to South Africa, Mozambique, Tanzania, Kenya, and Somalia, and on another trip to South America. In addition she has taken her quilting along on trips across Canada, Nova Scotia, Mexico, Alaska, and the backwoods of the Yukon.

"For me, quilting is a complete change of pace and a relaxing activity. My workbasket sits by my chair and lamp. I stitch as I listen to the news, et cetera. After all, I've seen John Chancellor and the Washington Monument before."

There have been no quilters in Elizabeth Garrison's family since the 1930s when her great-grandmother quilted. Now that Elizabeth has started, her sister has also been bitten by the quilting bug.

MATERIALS

8 colors, ⅝ yard of 45″ fabric for each color.
4¾ yards harmonizing color for the background. Each color is numbered in the Piecing Guide, which shows how the colors are arranged to get the lovely sunburst effect.

CUTTING GUIDE

Cut 64 pieces from figure 1 in each of the 8 colors (¼″ seam allowance *is* included).

ASSEMBLY

Assemble pieces in strips in the order indicated in the Piecing Guide. Sew 8 strips together to make 1 large diamond. This will be 1 of the 8 points of the large star. Complete the 7 remaining large diamonds, and join to form the star, leaving seams open ¼″ at the inner angles.

From the background color, cut 4 pieces 24¾″ square. Then cut 4 triangles from 2 pieces approximately 25⅛″ square. Because seams in the star may vary and affect the size of its sides, you need to measure the star carefully *before* cutting the corner squares and triangles. Lay your star flat on a table so the bias pieces don't stretch. Measure the side of the star from the inner angle to the point for the exact size of the side of the corner squares. Add ⅜″ to this measurement for the 2 squares that are to be cut into triangles. Stay-stitch the bias side of triangles ¼″ from each side of the cutting line before cutting.

Sew the triangles in first, then the square, sewing from the inner angle out to points. This makes a square quilt. Borders 8″ to 10″ on the ends will make it long enough to cover pillows.

Eight rows of diamonds the size of figure 1 will assemble into 1 point of an 8-pointed star to make a quilt about 80″ × 96″ inches for a double bed.

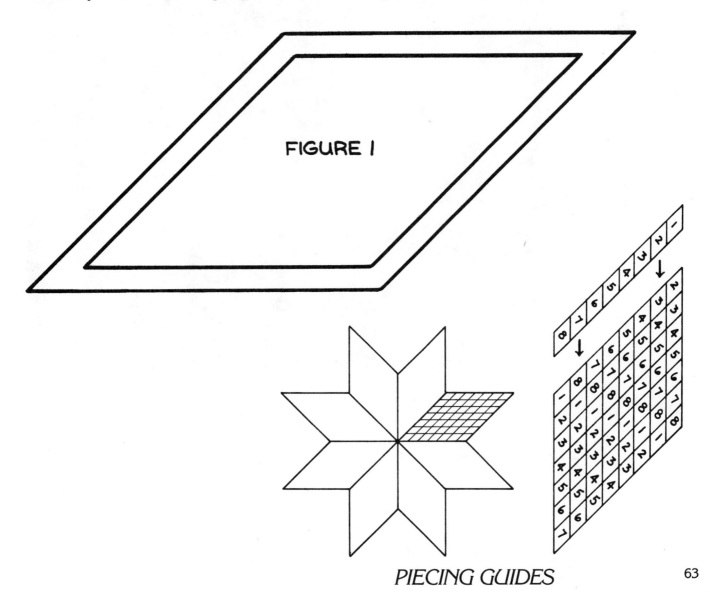

FIGURE 1

PIECING GUIDES   63

DORIS IWALANI FEARY NOSAKA · *Hilo, Hawaii*

MY BELOVED FLAG

*K*u'u Hae Aloha (My Beloved Flag) *represents a very important part of the rich history of Hawaii. At the time of the overthrow of the Hawaiian monarchy and the subsequent lowering of their flag, many Hawaiian people feared that they would not again be permitted to fly the emblem of their kingdom. They turned to quilting as a means of perpetuating the flag and the coat of arms—the result was* My Beloved Flag.

Castle Magic (© 1982) by Marguerite Zahoruiko, page 116. (PHOTO BY WILLIAM MAKRIS)

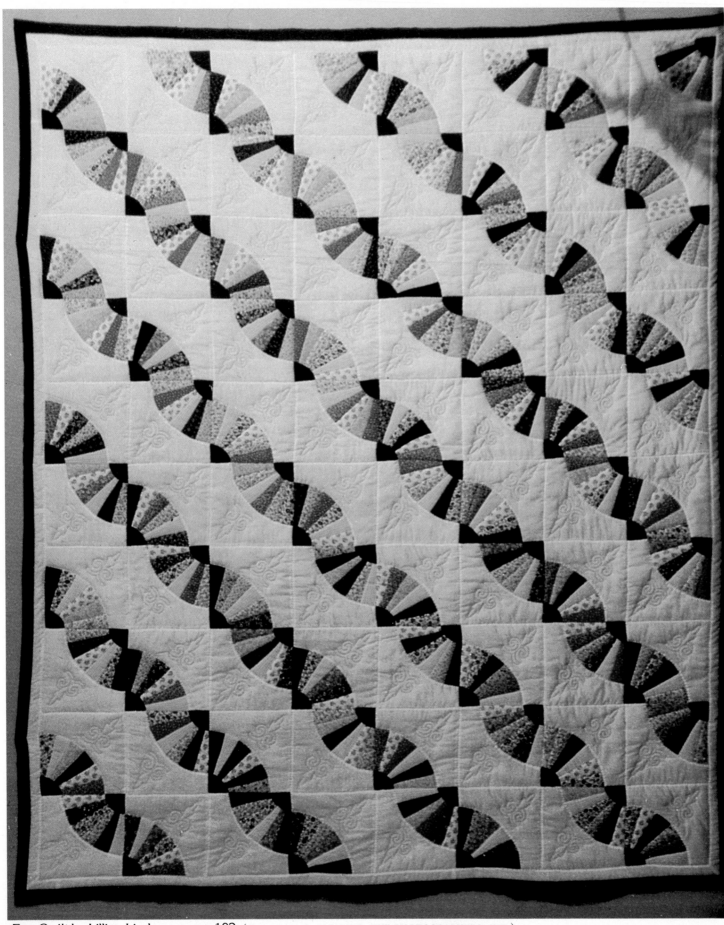

Fan Quilt by Lillian Lindgren, page 102. (PHOTO BY AL RUNNING, THE PHOTOGRAPHERS, INC.)

Maine Sampler Quilt by Cindy Taylor Clark (© 1979), page 88. (PHOTO BY CINDY TAYLOR CLARK)

Medallion Quilt by Gary W. Dean, page 108. (PHOTO BY DENNIS J. BELL)

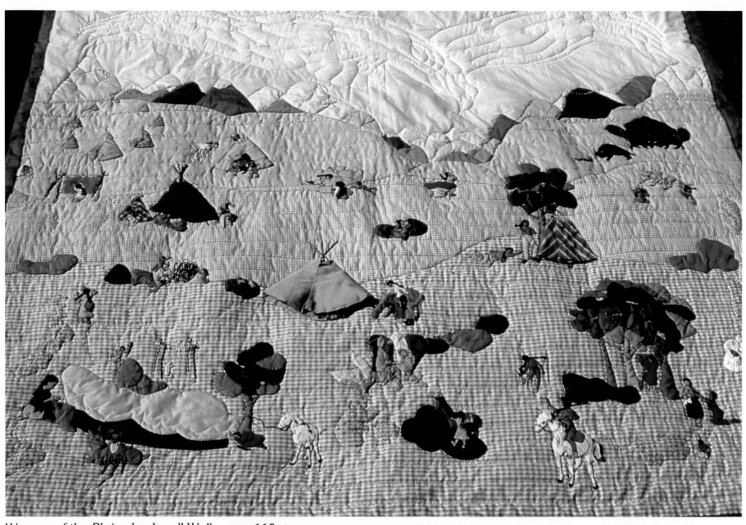

Women of the Plains by Jewell Wolk, page 110. (PHOTO BY RAYMOND R. PARKER)

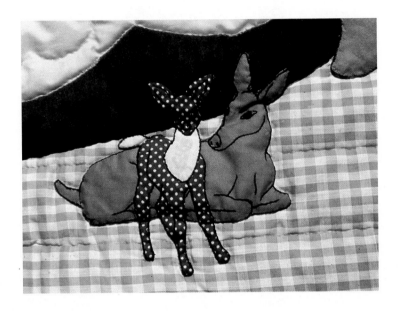

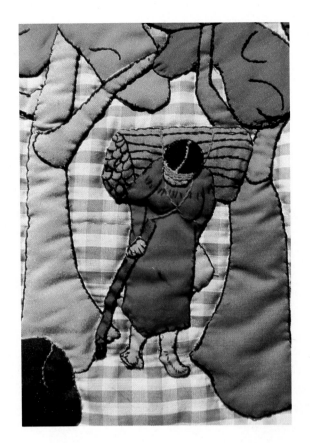

Sunburst by Yoko Sawanobori, page 90. (PHOTO BY YOMEI SAWANOBORI)

Doris Nosaka's Ku'u Hae Aloha has won Best Overall Quilt at
County Fair; Best Traditional, Best of Show and Most Original a
of Hawaii, King Kamehameha Celebration.

"Many Hawaiian flag quilts have been designed throughout
Each creator has a different approach to the interpretation of the in
pride in the solemnity of the subject matter so dear to our hearts. I
for any Hawaiian quiltmaker, this remains one of the more tradition
pieces to be worked on only when you have mastered the art of Hau
designing and quiltmaking. This particular design I envisioned in a
—thus the differences from any other Hawaiian flag. The name of the
is always the same, no matter who the quiltmaker is, although the
patterns of this almost sacred symbol of the Hawaiian people are varie
the quiltmaker. As you have probably guessed by now, no one is allou
to sit upon the quilt, as it would constitute something of a sacrilege to
so."

Doris, who grew up in a small community, was encouraged to lear
number of needlework skills—crocheting, embroidery, patchwork, and s
forth.

"Quilting was my particular favorite as I was allowed the freedom to
create my own designs. Also, since I was one of nine children with never
enough blankets to keep warm, quiltmaking would provide the necessary
comfort for the rest of my years."

The responsibilities of marriage and motherhood interrupted Doris'
quiltmaking. "But when my older children went off to school and my
youngest son was born, I attended a few refresher workshops and finally
found the time to work on and finish a sixteen-year-old original quilt I had
basted and stored away. Since then, twenty-eight years ago, I have found
the time to design and create, to teach and also to organize quilt clubs."

With its historical background and subject, this quilt is not the "typi-
cal" Hawaiian eight-point pattern. The four Union Jack colors (flags)
bordering the royal coat of arms were pieced together, then attached to the
center piece. Because of the bisymmetry of the coat of arms, the quilt has
a very definite top and bottom, unlike the eight-point designs.

Each part of the coat of arms was appliquéd onto the yellow background, then the colors (flags) were attached. To this completed top, the
batting and backing were basted together. This was put onto the quilting
sticks (attached to sawhorses) with dowel rods, then echo-quilted, beginning in the center, to approximately three inches from the coat of arms.
The quilting on the colors (flags) follows its own lines.

JOSEPH'S COAT

*T*wenty blocks, each an individual statement of color and design, make up this vivid quilt. The strong composition and exuberant colors combine to produce a fresh interpretation of a traditional quilt.

Joseph's Coat *won First Prize at the Idaho State Fair in the pieced and quilted category. This prizewinning quilt is made entirely of wool. Mrs. Linning likes to work with wool because of the bright colors available in wool, although she occasionally quilts in cotton.*

She has been quilting on and off for fifty years, but only began entering her work at the Idaho State Fair three years ago. Mrs. Linning has won a First Prize every year she has entered one of her quilts.

She is a self-taught quilter and the first in her family to quilt. Her advice to those just starting to quilt is "Practice."

Each of the blocks in this prizewinning quilt would make an outstanding quilt in itself.

MATERIALS

Assorted bright shades of wool fabric from skirts and sewing scraps.

CUTTING GUIDE

Quilt consists of twenty blocks 15″ square. Templates do *not* include seam allowances.

For each block, cut:

    Figure 1–1
    Figure 2–4
    Figure 3–4
    Figure 4–8 in a dark color
    Figure 4–8 in a light contrasting color
    Figure 5–32 in a light contrasting color
    Figure 5–4 in a dark contrasting color

For borders, cut strips 15½″ × 3″ (this measurement includes seam allowance), 24 in one color, 25 in a contrasting shade.

Small corner squares joining strips are 4 units of figure 4, in 2 contrasting colors: cut 60 pieces in each of two colors.

ASSEMBLY

The individual blocks are probably most easily pieced in diagonal strips; start with the long central strip and work outward according to Piecing Guide.

Finished blocks are set together in rows of 4, alternating with five 15″ strips. Last, join four 15″ strips in the contrasting color, with small pieced 3″ squares between each strip. There will be 6 of these long strips altogether. Join 1 row of 4 blocks to one of the border strips, then attach another border strip to the opposite long side. Attach the next set of 4 blocks to this border strip; then alternate adding borders and blocks until entire quilt top is joined.

A very slender binding completes the quilt after backing and batting have been added. Quilting follows the stitching lines, ¼″ inside all seams.

Depending on your binding treatment, your quilt will measure approximately 73″ × 91″.

Template Figures do not include seam allowance

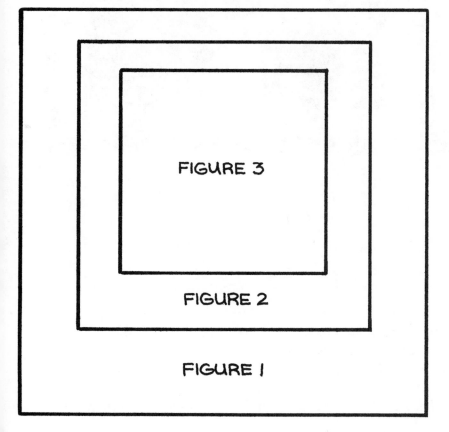

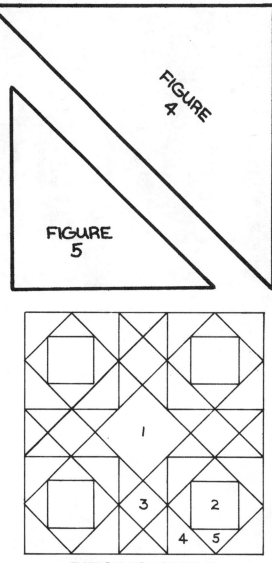

PIECING GUIDE

SHIRLEY FOMBY · *Mundelein, Illinois*

PATRONAGE OF THE ARTS

"It came to me in the night: a way to stop time and capture a few special years that would never again be repeated. My life was full of taxiing children to dance and music lessons, reminding them to practice, attending recitals, and sending countless checks to finance it all. And yet I knew all too soon it would be over. I decided to do something specific to remember it all."

That is how the idea for Patronage of the Arts *began. It was perfect timing, because Shirley Fomby received a contest flyer and saw an opportunity not only to capture her memories but to possibly win a prize as well. Her entry won First Prize in the National Grange Sewing Machine Craft and Home Decorating Contest in Illinois and went on to win First Prize at the national level.*

Shirley has been quilting "with a passion" for five years. Before that she had made a few quilts simply to use up scraps. She says of herself, "I am not a purist. I am more than willing to combine fabrics of different weights, finishes, and types to produce just the look I want. I generally use a polyester batt, but I do experiment with different weights."

"Finish what you start!" is her advice to beginners. "Begin small and then go on to something larger. In this way you get your feet wet and learn technique before committing yourself to a full-size quilt."

Patronage of the Arts *is an innovative blend of piecing, hand and machine appliqué and quilting. Because this quilt was designed as a wall hanging (and therefore was not meant to be laundered) the quilter has greater flexibility in materials and techniques.*

Shirley used many different materials to give the quilt a three-dimensional look, using velveteen for the curtain; gold metallic trim for the tieback of the curtain; white taffeta for the piano keyboard; a non-ravel suede for the keys; and Mylar fabric for the stage lights. The finished piece is 34" × 50".

Meticulous attention to detail gives this quilt its unique personalized style. For example, Shirley hand-gathered the fabric of the little girls' dresses to give a fluffy look and added a bit of color to their cheeks with pink tailor's chalk.

Guitar chords, copied from a book for accuracy, are machine-stitched and hand-embroidered. The stage lights are machine-stitched, and a glue stick was handy to hold them in place while stitching. Before stitching the curtain down, gold metallic trim was added as a tieback. The string-pieced multicolor border of "sound" is pieced onto fabric 2½" wide and the length of each side of the quilt for an even but random distribution of color.

Hand-embroidered dedication, signature and date in the lower right corner complete the piece.

EXPERIMENT IN HARMONY

*E*xperiment in Harmony *is a pictorial history of the experimental community of New Harmony, Indiana, a favorite place of quilter Marilyn Price. She spent a great deal of time researching the history of this unique community before starting her quilt and now visits the town regularly.*

Among the awards this piece has won is First Prize at the Indiana State Fair in the professional fine arts/crafts category. This quilt resulted in several commissions for the prizewinner.

Marilyn has been quilting for about ten years. Her work is in many private collections throughout the country as well as in the Indianapolis Museum of Art. Her mother and grandmother both quilted and Marilyn credits her early exposure to this art form for her interest in continuing the tradition.

One unusual aspect of this quilt is the silkscreen designs onto which Marilyn appliquéd her figures.

A silkscreen is a wooden frame covered with a fine-mesh silk (sometimes a fine Dacron can be substituted). On this screen, areas are masked so that they do not permit ink to pass through onto the fabric being printed. There are different ways to mask an area: a light-sensitive film can be painted on the screen in areas that are to be blocked out; or a stencil can be cut and attached to the screen.

After the screen has been set up and the appropriate areas blocked, a squeegee forces the ink through the screen, and the image, defined by the masked areas, is transferred onto the fabric positioned below the screen.

Materials for silkscreening are available at most art supply stores and paint stores. There are numerous books on the subject, which is frequently offered in adult education classes.

This quilt was designed first in pencil sketches made from research material accumulated through reading about and visiting New Harmony. The images were silkscreened on polished cotton. Appliqué and embroidery came next. Quilting by machine and hand followed.

The finished piece is 4' × 7'.

EVELYN RAPPATH · *Roseville, Minnesota and*
EUNICE R. LOOTS · *Gowrie, Iowa*

MINNESOTA
WILD DUCK QUILT

*T*he Minnesota Wild Duck Quilt *is not only a family effort by two sisters, Evelyn Rappath and Eunice Loots, but an interstate accomplishment.*

Evelyn lives in Minnesota and her sister Eunice in Iowa. When Evelyn's son, an avid hunter, was asked what he wanted for a fortieth-birthday present, he said he'd like a bedspread with wild ducks. He had no sympathy for his mother when she replied that she knew nothing about wild ducks.

"Go to the library," he said, and so she did. At the library she sketched wild ducks. Later, she looked for fabric that would represent the colors of the ducks. The ponds were made out of her husband's old shirts.

Because Evelyn still works, her sister Eunice offered to quilt her nephew's present after Evelyn had pieced the top.

Quilting is a tradition in Evelyn and Eunice's family. Their mother, aunts, and grandmother all made quilts.

MATERIALS

Beige cotton fabric for background, medium brown cotton for borders, cream cotton for appliquéd blocks, deep brown cotton and multicolored scraps and remnants for appliqué work. Brown wool embroidery yarn is used for detail.

CUTTING GUIDE

Measurements *include* ¼" seam allowance.

Cut twelve 10½" squares from cream cotton.

Cut 15 strips 3" × 10½" and three 14½" squares from the beige. For borders, cut from beige 1 piece 62" × 22" and 2 pieces 154" × 22".

Cut twenty-four 3" squares from deep brown.

Cut 24 strips 10½" × 2½" and 24 strips 14½" × 2½" of the medium brown cotton.

ASSEMBLY

This quilt is composed of 12 appliquéd blocks and 3 plain blocks with lattice and border. The three plain blocks are tucked under the pillows. To assemble, first complete appliqué and embroidery work. Using original drawings or tracings from books (see examples shown), trace outline of duck and pond and, using various earth-tone fabrics, cut and assemble pieces for individual ducks and ponds. Appliqué onto cream squares, and finish with embroidered naturalistic details, such as grasses and cattails. Embroider the duck's species below his pond, if desired.

Once all 12 blocks have been completed, attach two 10½" × 2½" strips and two 14½" × 2½" strips to each block, to create 14" blocks. Then attach 1 block to lattice strips and squares, and complete one row of 3 blocks in this manner. Repeat for all remaining blocks, including plain blocks. Join strips to form the quilt top, positioning the row of plain blocks second from the top. Then join the borders, beginning with the sides, and then attach the border to the bottom of the quilt. The borders were made wide enough for the quilt to cover a queen-size bed.

Quilting follows seam lines, except in the border, which is quilted in a crosshatch pattern that is added after the quilt is in the frame.

Pintail Duck

Wood Duck

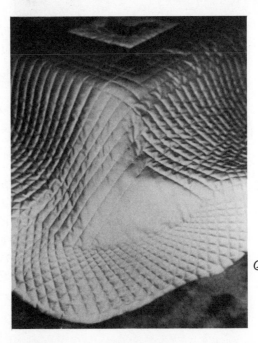

Quilting

73

CHRIS WOLF EDMONDS · *Lawrence, Kansas*

CHEROKEE TRAIL OF TEARS

*I*n the winter of 1838–39, President Andrew Jackson, who had no sympathy for the plight of the Indians, ordered "the great removal." Of the sixteen thousand Cherokee who were driven from their homes by federal troops, more than four thousand died along the way from disease, hunger, and exposure. The march lasted nearly a year and ever after it was known as "The Trail Where They Cried."

Cherokee Trail of Tears *(© 1979)* is a highly stylized and imaginative creation, combining traditional patterns (the modified Bear Paw border and running wave) with contemporary appliqué. The quilting is an all-over diamond pattern.

Chris Edmonds was inspired to create this evocative quilt after seeing contemporary Cherokee art relating to this traumatic chapter of Native American history. She set out to depict the hope and despair of the Cherokee nation, and succeeded brilliantly.

Cherokee Trail of Tears *won Best of Show at the International Quilt Contest, Del Mar, California.*

Chris is a self-taught quilter who relates: "Like all families which go back many generations in this country, my family quilted of necessity. While both my mother and grandmother are fine seamstresses, they are of the generation that quilting skipped, for the most part, because of machine-made bedding."

Chris has not only mastered the art of quilting, she also designs patterns and lectures extensively. To the neophyte quilter, she suggests, "Try a variety of techniques to find the ones that work best for you, and strive for creative design and color."

The figures on the quilt symbolize the heritage of the Cherokee nation. The seated figure (based on a Willard Stone sculpture) represents the despair of the "Trail of Tears." The figures of the woman and child represent the struggle to survive the journey to a new land and a new life. Above this is the figure of Sequoya with quill raised, to represent the hope of the future. The bird at the top is the legendary phoenix, which represents the ability of the great Cherokee nation to rejuvenate itself after tragedy. The border is original in design, but bears a resemblance to the traditional quilt pattern Indian Chief. The seven-point star in the upper right corner is from the seal of the Cherokee nation and represents the seven ancient clans, the legendary beginnings of the Cherokee people.

The Cherokee nation was the only Indian tribe to have its own alphabet, enabling the Cherokee to read and write in their own language. The quilting in the top border and the bottom border are symbols from this eighty-five-character alphabet.

FEDERAL HILL FEATHER

*P*olly Smith's Federal Hill Feather *was one of twelve outstanding Kentucky quilts to be featured in the 1983 Kentucky Quilt Calendar. It has won First Prize at the Montgomery County Fair and the Kentucky State Fair, as well as numerous other awards.*

*"The original quilt from which this has been reproduced (*Princess Feather, c. 1820*) was made for the famous residence of Judge John Rowan, by his mother, Eliza Cooper Rowan. Among the many notable people who were entertained in Judge Rowan's home was his young cousin Stephen Foster, who immortalized the home in 1853 with the publication of his song "My Old Kentucky Home."*

Polly was approached in the 1970s to reproduce the quilt as part of a program to improve and expand the merchandise sold in state park gift shops. At that time, she felt the quilt was too difficult, but she changed her mind as her skills improved. She began to work in 1980 and finished it in early 1982.

Just finding fabric in colors to match the pattern was difficult, and Polly finally persuaded a wholesale mail order firm to sell her yardage (instead of full bolts) of the needed material.

A good friend and expert quiltmaker, Sarah Ann Means, helped take the pattern from the original 1820 quilt but Polly did the actual construction and quilting.

Polly has been quilting for about twenty-eight years. "Quilting is not a tradition in my family, but being raised during the Depression, I was taught to be conservative. I can remember old blankets being covered with fabric and tied to make them last another year or so."

Of a Double Wedding Ring quilt she made, Polly said, "I proceeded to piece this on the sewing machine and did quite an admirable job, only later to be told that it was impossible to piece this pattern by machine. I guess that I have proven everyone wrong on the techniques that I employ in quiltmaking, such as doing frameless quilting. I do lap quilting or table-top quilting—starting in the middle and quilting out like the spokes of a wheel. I started with the large frame, but it took up too much space in our small house. I tried the hoops, but they were frustrating, and I got mad one day and threw them across the room and broke them."

Polly, who has been entering quilt contests for twenty-five years tells new quilters, "Stay with it! Don't get discouraged . . . you cannot sit down and play the piano at your first attempt; it takes years to develop a skill, and to do this you have to practice, practice, and practice. Quilt, quilt, and more quilting."

MATERIALS

All-cotton fabrics in red, green, and gold prints. Unbleached muslin for background and backing.

CUTTING GUIDE

Templates include seam allowance for hand-appliquéing. Seam allowance should be added to background and border measurements.

From background fabric, cut:
    4–36" squares
    2–12" × 72" borders
    2–12" × 96" borders
From print fabric, cut:
    16–red feathers
    16–green feathers
    4–small yellow stars
    4–small red stars
    4–yellow centers

    1–large yellow flower
    1–red star
    1–yellow center

    40–green vines, or use a bias
   200–green leaves
    40–red flowers
    40–yellow centers

ASSEMBLY

Begin with the 4 squares of the quilt, working with 1 at a time. Place a central star on the center point of the square and place the feathers in a pleasing arrangement. Baste the star loosely first and then slip the feathers under the star. Baste feathers, turning under edges of all pieces and clipping curves as needed. Each square can then be completely appliquéd with a blind stitch on all pieces.

Next join all 4 squares and place the center design at the point where the 4 squares meet.

Then add the borders. The appliqué is traced on, and then stitched to the border.

The batting and back are added, and binding is used to complete the quilt.

The quilting designs are then traced onto the quilt top according to the placement indicated on the Quilting Designs. Additionally, the appliquéd motifs are outlined with quilting. The 8-leaf flower is quilted ½" inside the appliqué twice, as well as around the outside edge.

Polly notes that if she were to quilt *Federal Hill Feather* again, she would quilt down through the middle of each feather appliqué and into the small tips. The original quilt was *not* quilted this way but she feels that this additional quilting would make the quilt design lie flatter. In addition to the feather wreaths, scrolls, and plume quilting designs, the background is stipple- or echo-quilted ¼" apart.

The finished quilt measures 92" × 92".

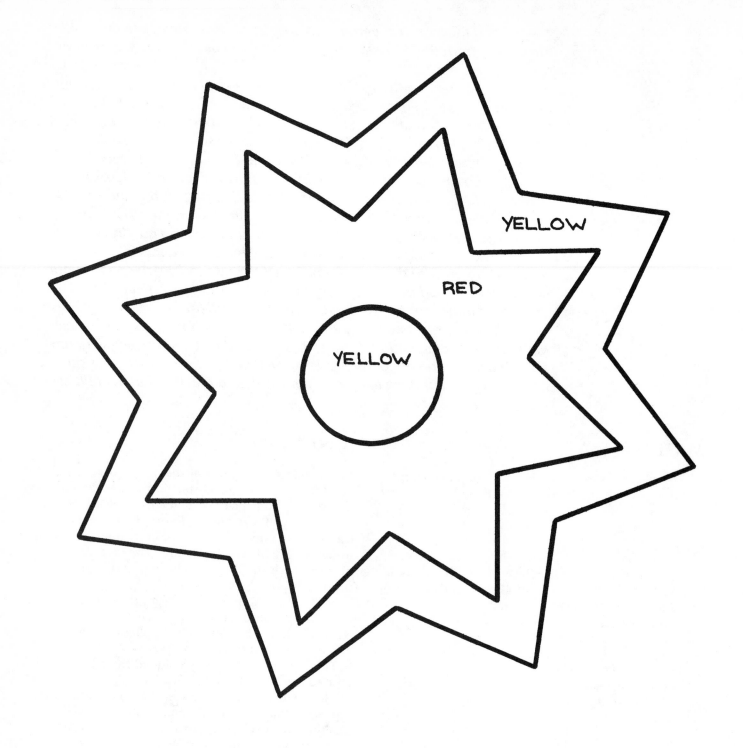

APPLIQUÉ FIGURES

YELLOW

RED

GREEN

GREEN

APPLIQUÉ FIGURES

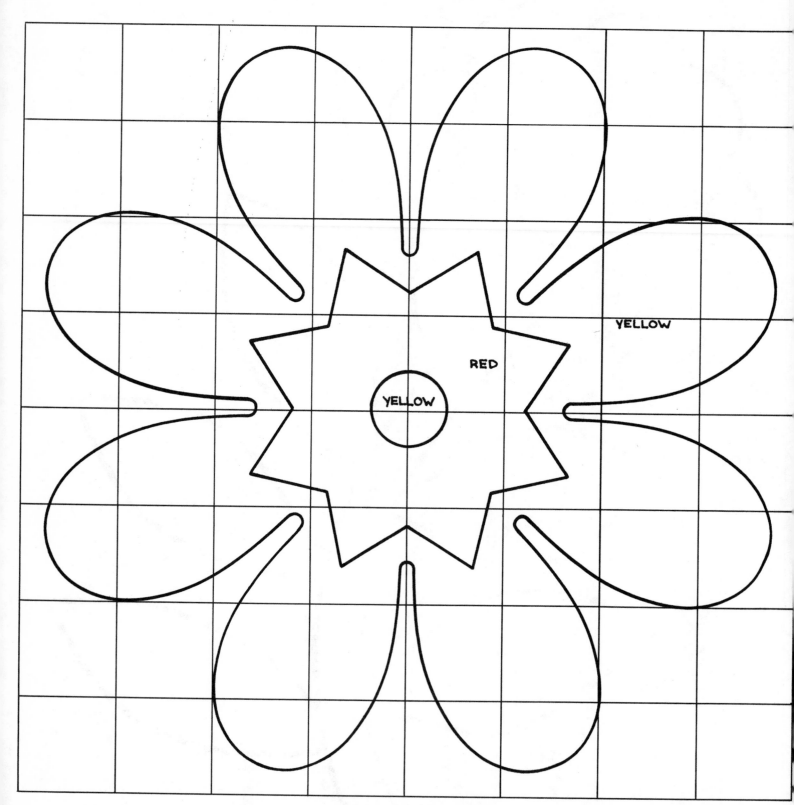

APPLIQUÉ FIGURES

(shown at 50 percent of full size; use the graph lines to enlarge to full size)

QUILTING DESIGNS

APPLIQUÉ FIGURE

81

(shown at 50 percent of full size; use the graph lines to enlarge to full size)

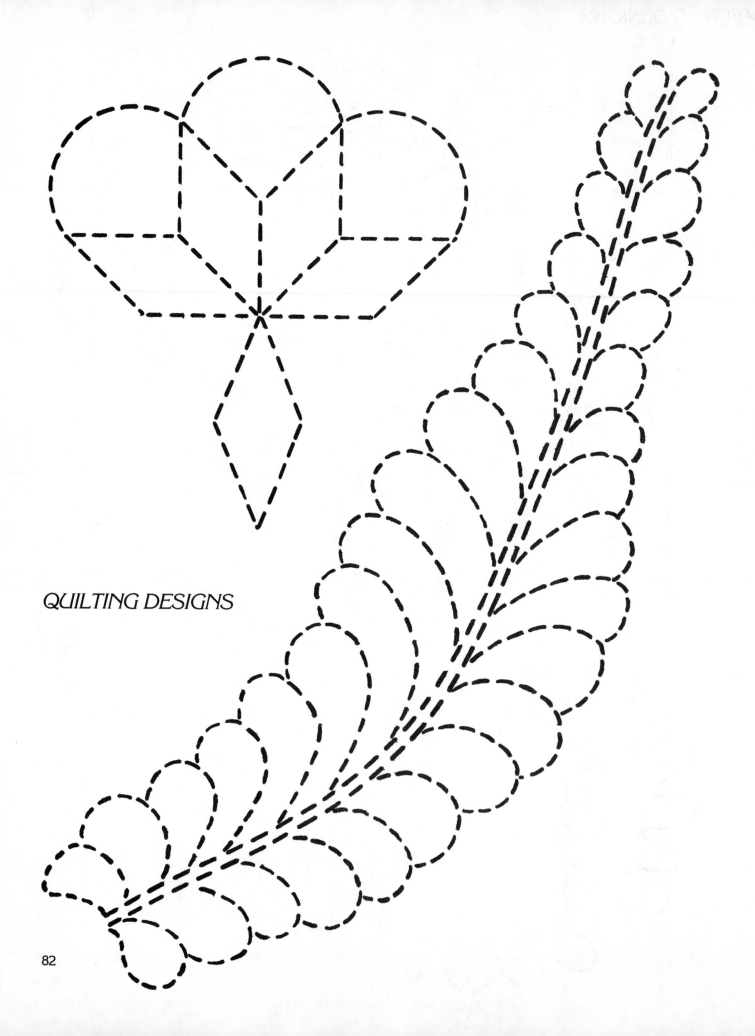

QUILTING DESIGNS

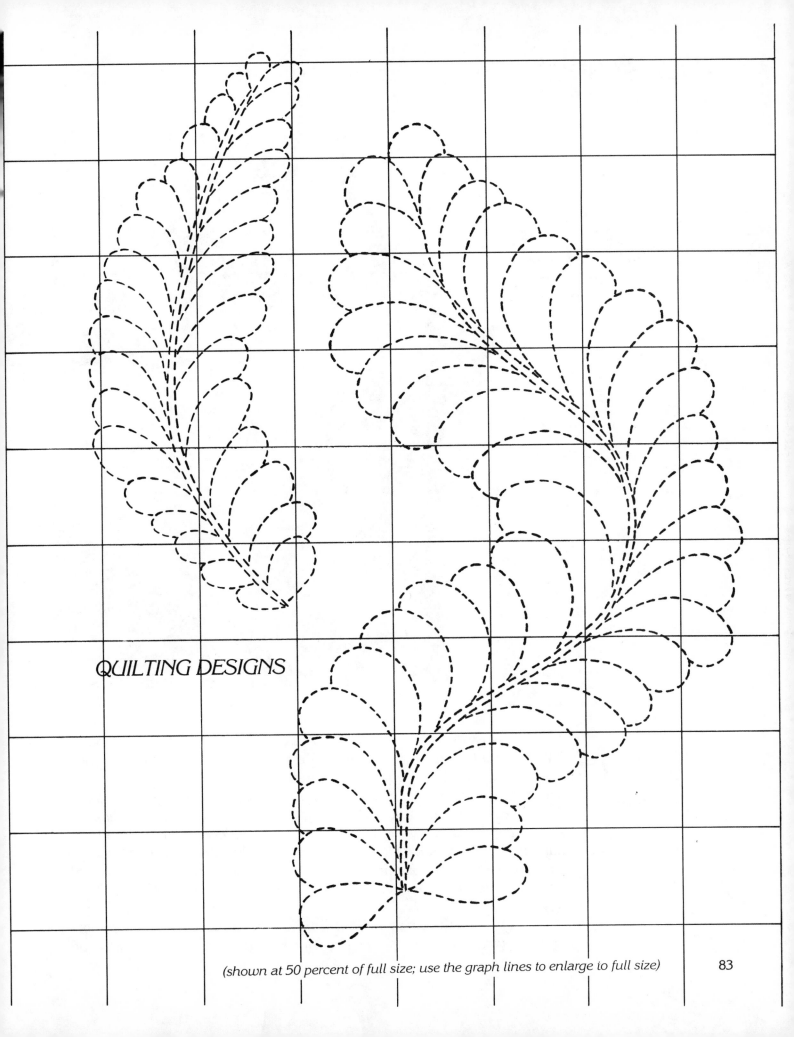

QUILTING DESIGNS

(shown at 50 percent of full size; use the graph lines to enlarge to full size)   83

SUBTLE
STAR

R ose Sanders relates the following story about her first quilting venture:
"When I first began to quilt, there was no one around I could turn to for
questions or advice. I read in a book that seven stitches per inch was
acceptable for quilting. I was quilting my first pieced quilt, Star of Blue-
grass. With some frustration and after a couple of months' work, I finally
succeeded. My son, joining in the excitement, noticed that I had the hem
gauge set on centimeters instead of inches; I was actually quilting eighteen
stitches to an inch! And this was counting the top stitching only. Normally,
I now put eleven to fourteen stitches per inch, depending on the quilt
design."

Subtle Star was given its name by Rose because of its muted colors
and innovative border, which she designed. It has collected a number of

awards, including a Blue Ribbon and "Margaret Burks' Award" (best quilting stitch) at the Patchwork Pelican Quilt Show, Baton Rouge, Louisiana; a Blue Ribbon and "Founders' Award" in the South/Southwest Houston Quilt Show; and for two years in a row it has won the award for best execution of quilting stitches at the National Quilt Association Show.

Rose's advice to quilters is, "Read, listen, and digest. What is known as a difficult pattern may often be a most rewarding experience."

Since she prefers traditional quilts, 100 percent cotton is a fabric must for her. Rose also prefers cotton batting for a traditional look and feel.

Rose has only been quilting for six years and entered her first show in 1981.

MATERIALS

Unbleached muslin for background and small printed 100 percent cotton for contrast. Cotton batting.

CUTTING GUIDE

The templates do *not* include seam allowances. There are 12 blocks 13" square with pieced stars.

For each of these blocks cut:
    Figure 1–1 print
    Figure 2–4 muslin
    Figure 3–8 print
    Figure 4–8 print
    Figure 5–8 muslin
    Figure 6–48 muslin
    Figure 6–24 print
    Figure 7–4 muslin
For the borders, cut:
    2 borders 9" × 72"
    2 borders 9" × 92"
    Figure 8–14 print
    Figure 9–4 print
    Figure 10–18 print
For the background, cut:
    6 plain muslin 13" blocks
    10 plain muslin triangles (called half-blocks), ½ of 13" blocks
    4 plain muslin corner triangles (called quarter-blocks), ¼ of 13" block

ASSEMBLY

To assemble pieced blocks, the design for each block is broken down into 9 equal parts. For each of the 9 smaller squares begin by sewing together the smallest pieces in strips, which then are attached to the larger piece(s) along a straight seam. This avoids having to sew into corners.

When the 8 small units, plus a plain square for center, have been completed, stitch 3 units in a row and then join the 3 rows to form a square. This completes 1 pieced block. Proceed to complete all 12 pieced blocks.

When all the blocks are completed, arrange the entire quilt top on a flat surface (a table or floor). Pieced blocks should alternate with plain muslin blocks; the half-blocks and quarter-blocks should be fitted in at the ends and corners. Proceed to sew these together in diagonal strips; then join all the strips to form a complete quilt top.

Next add the borders and the appliqué of the borders. When this is completed, the cotton batting and muslin backing can be attached.

The background is horizontally quilted with straight stitches (except for the top and bottom half-blocks, which are vertically stitched). In contrast, the borders are diagonally stitched. All seam lines are outlined ¼" from the stitching. A large floral motif is quilted into the plain blocks.

The finished quilt measures 72" × 92".

Template Figures do not include seam allowance

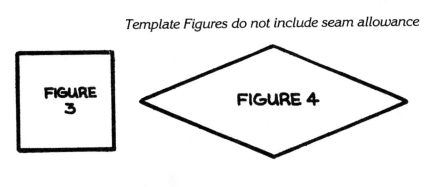

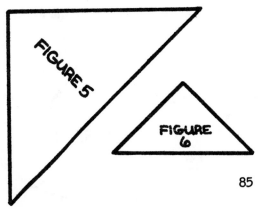

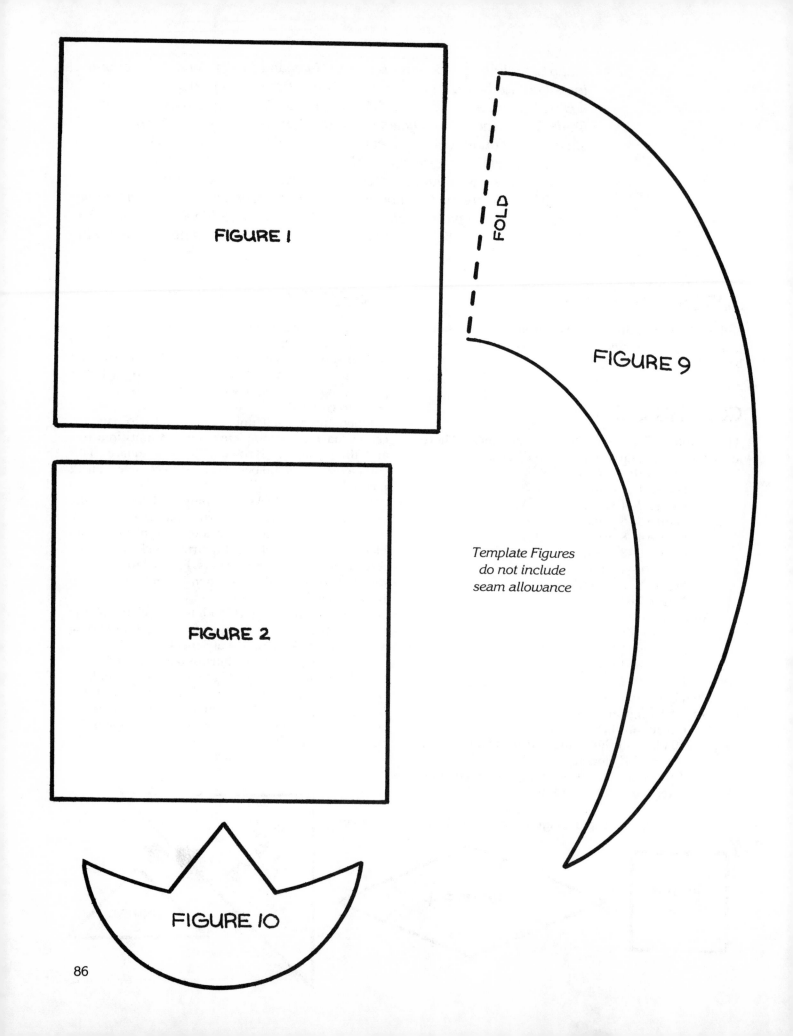

FIGURE 1

FIGURE 2

FOLD

FIGURE 9

Template Figures
do not include
seam allowance

FIGURE 10

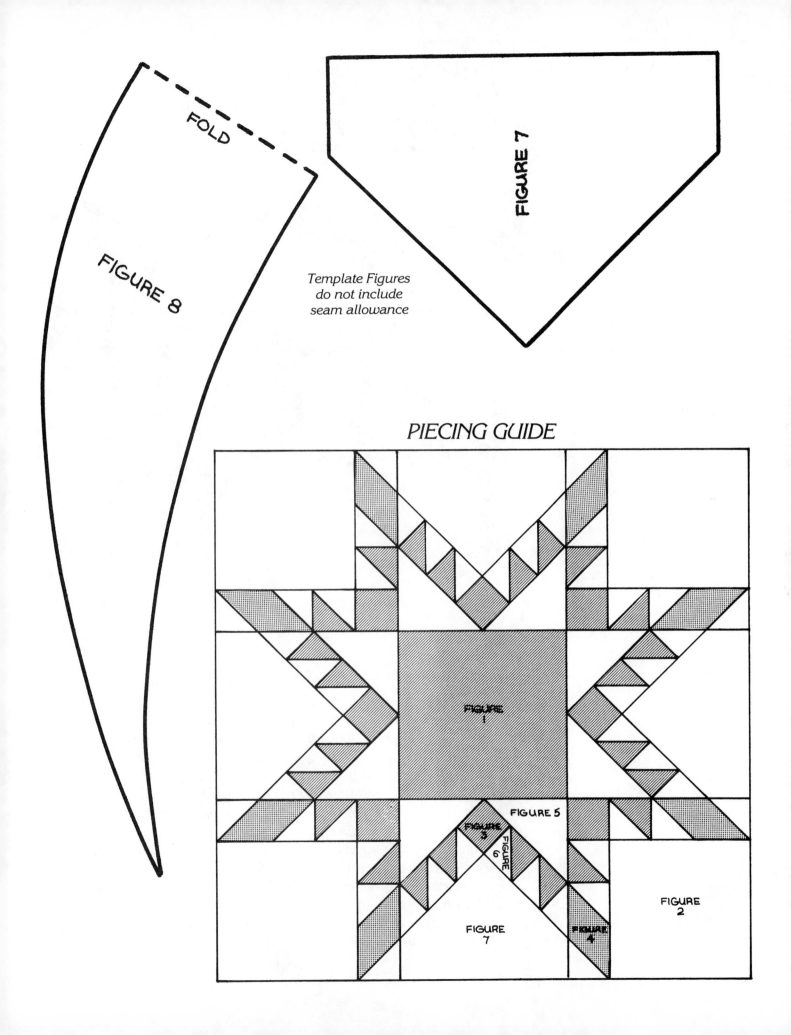

FOLD

FIGURE 8

FIGURE 7

*Template Figures
do not include
seam allowance*

PIECING GUIDE

FIGURE 1

FIGURE 2

FIGURE 3

FIGURE 4

FIGURE 5

FIGURE 6

FIGURE 7

MAINE SAMPLER QUILT

© 1979

*T*his bright, fresh sampler features nine blocks in vivid red, blue, white, and gold with complementary prints in the same colors. Samplers have had a surge of popularity in recent years. They are an excellent first project for beginners and a wonderful way for the veteran quilter to use up spare quilt blocks. Because of the proliferation of samplers, it is all the more exciting to find such a delightful, well-planned, and cheerful example.

The Maine Sampler Quilt (© 1979) was developed by Cindy Taylor Clark as a teaching tool because it includes a variety of patchwork and appliqué blocks with borders. Cindy's quilt has gone on to win First Prize in the hand-quilting category at the Franconia (New Hampshire) Quilt show. Most of the blocks are her original designs.

Her great-aunts and great-grandmother were quilters, but Cindy didn't begin to quilt until 1971 when she took an adult education class. She doesn't generally enter contests but does show her work at events she attends or at courses she teaches.

"I feel that for the 'quilt-as-you-go' method to be successful, you must make sure the individual blocks or rows are well basted to keep the work as flat as possible. This will eliminate "bunching" or having areas between quilting designs, which often distinguishes a traditionally made quilt from one done quilt-as-you-go! You don't want anyone to be able to tell the difference on the front of the quilt."

She used a 14" hoop to quilt most of the blocks, and quilted the borders by the lap method.

Cindy uses 100 percent cotton fabrics and both cotton and Dacron batting, but plans to experiment with silk and wool fabrics in the future.

Because of their manageability, quilt-as-you-go quilts have become more popular. In the quilt-as-you-go method, each block is completed individually, including the quilting. That is, the piecing of the top of the block is sewn first, then the batting and back of the block are attached. The quilting is also worked into the block. The next block is assembled from start to finish just like the first one. After all blocks have been finished, they are sewn together. The quilt is complete except for the border(s) and binding. One of the advantages of this type of quilting is that it can be successfully managed with just a hoop, rather than a large quilting frame. Another appealing factor is that each completed block gives the quilter a sense of accomplishment that is especially important for the beginner.

This method of quilting also makes adapting or changing a large or small quilt pattern easy. The quilter can make the necessary adjustments to fit the needs of a specific quilt size in many ways: adding more blocks; altering the size of the blocks; adding another border; or reducing borders, et cetera.

Detail showing piecing and quilting designs

© 1979

SUNBURST

*T*he quilting design of Yoko Sawanobori's Sunburst was inspired by the cloudlike design in the fabric used for the border. This unusual blue-and-white cotton fabric was purchased by Yoko's teenage daughter Tina on a visit to Japan.

It is a summer kimono fabric called Yukata, and the width of material is only 13½ inches. The blocks of the quilt were pieced by Yoko and her friends who call themselves the Mini Group. They have pieced ten quilts so far.

Sunburst took First Place in Group Quilts at the National Quilting Association, 1981, and was Grand Champion at the Maryland State Fair the same year. Yoko did all the quilting after she and her friends had pieced the blocks.

While on a visit to Japan, Yoko demonstrated quilting to many aspiring quilters in her native country. They were reluctant to use kimono fabric because of the strong traditional and religious connotations of these

garments. Though the quilt was admired, it also stunned her audience, because Yoko had used two kimono fabrics: the larger print is traditionally for a woman's garment; the smaller printed fabric is traditionally for a man's garment. As a quilter who sees the potential in unusual fabrics, Yoko could not let this beautiful material go unused. Since her lifestyle in the United States does not give her an opportunity to wear kimonos, she did what has been done traditionally; she used clothing to make quilts.

Yoko came to the U.S. many years ago to study nursing and stayed to marry and raise a family. She credits one of her fellow nurses for introducing her to the joys of quilting.

Like most quilters, she leads a busy life filled with family and professional responsibilities and hobbies, such as tennis and bridge, but she always finds the time to quilt.

MATERIALS

100 percent cotton, indigo blue, summer kimono fabrics in two prints. 1½ kimonos were used: Each was 13½" wide and 16 yards long. 1 yard of white 100 percent cotton fabric for piecing.

CUTTING GUIDE

Measurements and templates do *not* include seam allowance.

All borders and figure A are cut from one of the kimono fabrics, a blue-and-white larger-print fabric. From this fabric, cut:
Figure A—19
2 borders 7" × 76"
2 borders 6" × 100½"
3 borders 3½" × 64"
8 borders 3½" × 19"
For each block, from the white fabric, cut:
Figure B—16
Figure D—16
Figure F—32
Figure G—4
For each block, from the blue-and-white smaller-print fabric, cut:
Figure C—16
Figure E—32

ASSEMBLY

Join figures B, C, D into a "ring" in this order: B to C, D to C, then C again.

Next join figure A (circle) to this ring.

Piece together 32 each of figures E and F into another ring. When completed, stitch to joined section of figures A, B, C, and D. This completes one sunburst.

Next join 4 pieces of figure G together to make a hollow ring. Join the figure G ring to the pieced sunburst portion carefully.

Proceed to complete all blocks. Then attach in 4 rows of 3 with 3½" × 19" borders in between. When the 4 rows have all been joined, complete the quilt top by stitching together the rows with borders of 3½" × 64". The outside borders can then be attached. Top and bottom borders are 7" wide and side borders are 6" wide.

Quilting is ½" from seam line in the sunburst, following the piecing. For the white background fabric a sunbeam quilting effect was used, starting at the edge of the sunburst and working outward to the edge of the block.

Because of the unusual pattern of the borders, no quilting was done there.

The finished quilt measures 76" × 100½".

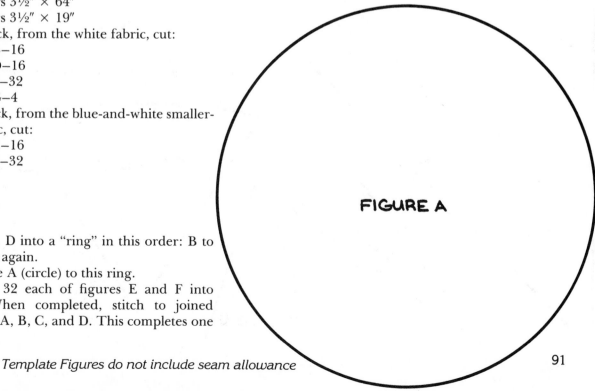

FIGURE A

Template Figures do not include seam allowance

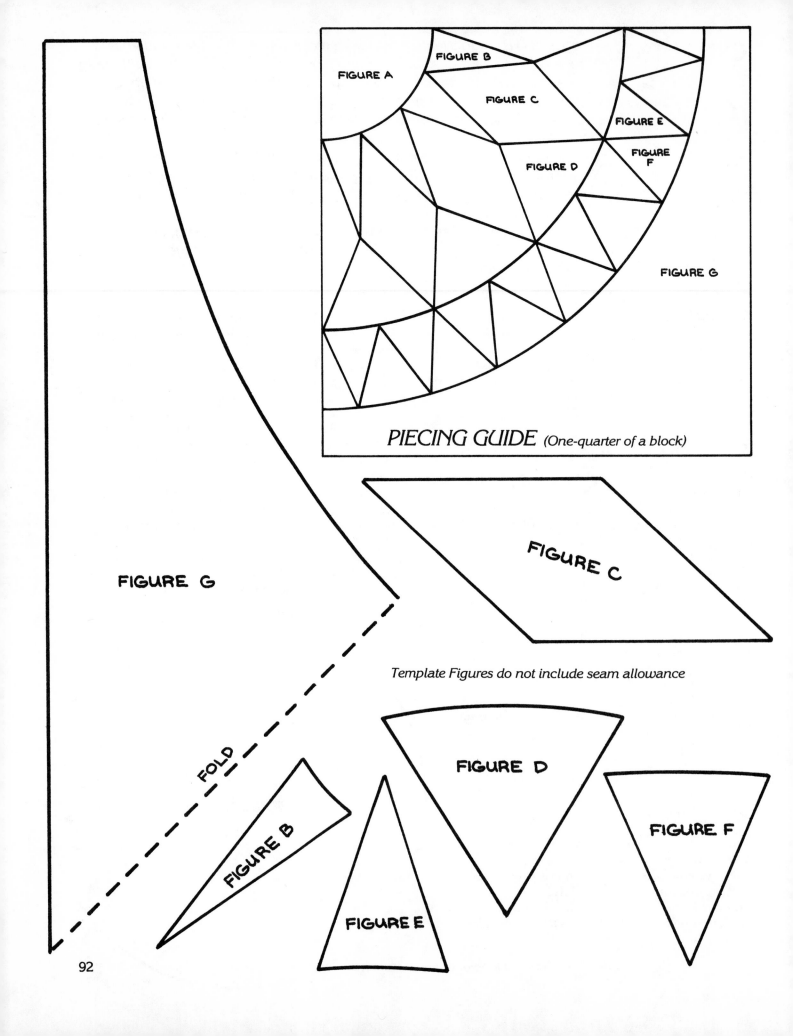

PIECING GUIDE *(One-quarter of a block)*

FIGURE A

FIGURE B

FIGURE C

FIGURE E

FIGURE F

FIGURE D

FIGURE G

FIGURE G

FIGURE C

Template Figures do not include seam allowance

FOLD

FIGURE B

FIGURE D

FIGURE F

FIGURE E

92

A PARTRIDGE IN A PEAR TREE

*T*his charming quilt with its festive green, red, white, and gold fabrics was
designed and made by Cynthia Shepard as a gift to her son for his first
Christmas. A Partridge in a Pear Tree *won First Prize in the patchwork and
appliqué, hand-quilted category of the Eastern States Exposition. This was
Cynthia's first entry in a quilt competition.*

*"I took quilting classes and workshops, but my quilting actually
started with my paternal great-grandmother. She was a quilter, as well as
a fine seamstress, and when she came to America from England she
supported herself with her needlework skills."*

*Cynthia's suggestions to beginners is, "Wash and dry all fabrics before
cutting. Take great pains to draw accurate patterns. Cut each piece individually."*

MATERIALS

1½ yards white cotton
2¾ yards red print
¼ yard green print
Scraps of red, green, and gold prints, and red
and green solids for appliqué

CUTTING GUIDE

Cut appliqué pieces from scraps according to Appliqué Figures; ¼" seam allowances *are* included on all
templates and measurements.
    From white fabric, cut:
        One 15" square for center block

Figure 21–32 for second border
Four 6½" squares for third border
4 borders 6½" × 26½" for third border
From red print fabric, cut:
Figure 6–2
Figure 7–1
Figure 8–1
Figure 9–1
2 strips 20½" × 3½" and 2 strips 15" × 3½"
    for first border
2 strips 3¼" × 38½" and 2 strips 3¼" × 45"
    for fourth border
2 pieces 26½" × 49" for backing
From gold print fabric, cut:
Figure 10–2
Figure 11–2
Figure 12–4
Figure 13–4
From either solid color or tiny red print, cut:
Figure 14–1
Figure 15–2
Figure 16–2
Figure 17–2
Figure 18–4
Figure 19–4
Figure 20–4
From green print fabric, cut:
Figure 1–1
Figure 2–2
Figure 3–2
Figure 4–2
Figure 5–2
Figure 21–32 for second border

ASSEMBLY

Appliqué pieces to 15" center square according to pattern. Appliqué smaller partridge motifs to 6½" squares and set aside. Attach first border in red print fabric to center block.

Piece triangles (figure 21) and attach second border in strips.

Join small appliquéd squares to white strips and attach to quilt top to form third border.

Last, attach fourth border, and press quilt top.

Stitch 2 backing pieces together and press. Baste quilt top, batting, and backing together. Mark quilt top with quilting designs: hearts for central square and inside border; partridge motifs for large white border (see Quilting Designs). Pieced and appliquéd work is quilted ¼" inside seam lines.

Trim backing to within ¾" of quilt top. Fold over and blind-stitch. Miter corners.

The finished quilt measures 45" × 45".

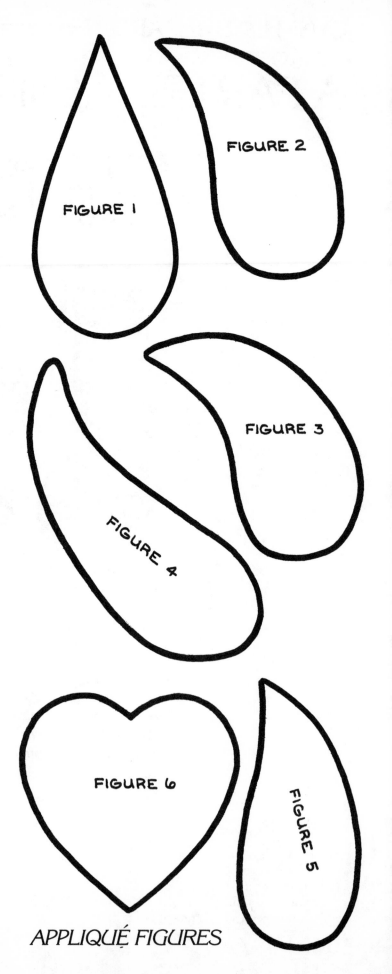

APPLIQUÉ FIGURES

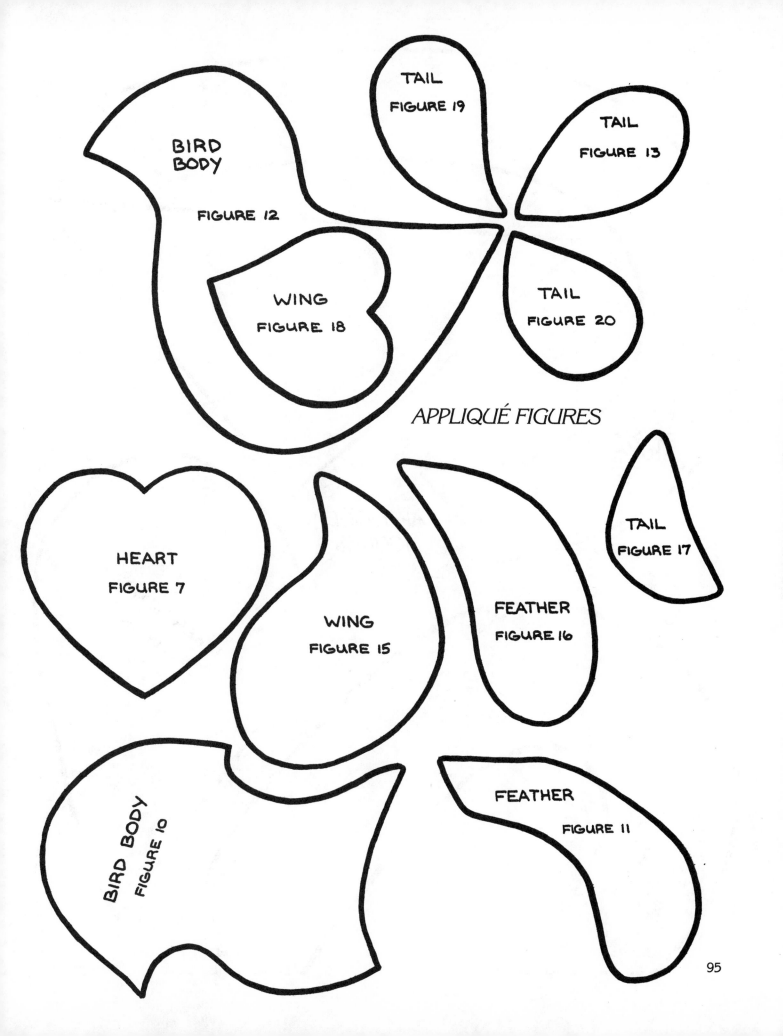

TAIL
FIGURE 19

TAIL
FIGURE 13

BIRD
BODY

FIGURE 12

WING
FIGURE 18

TAIL
FIGURE 20

APPLIQUÉ FIGURES

TAIL
FIGURE 17

HEART
FIGURE 7

WING
FIGURE 15

FEATHER
FIGURE 16

BIRD BODY
FIGURE 10

FEATHER
FIGURE 11

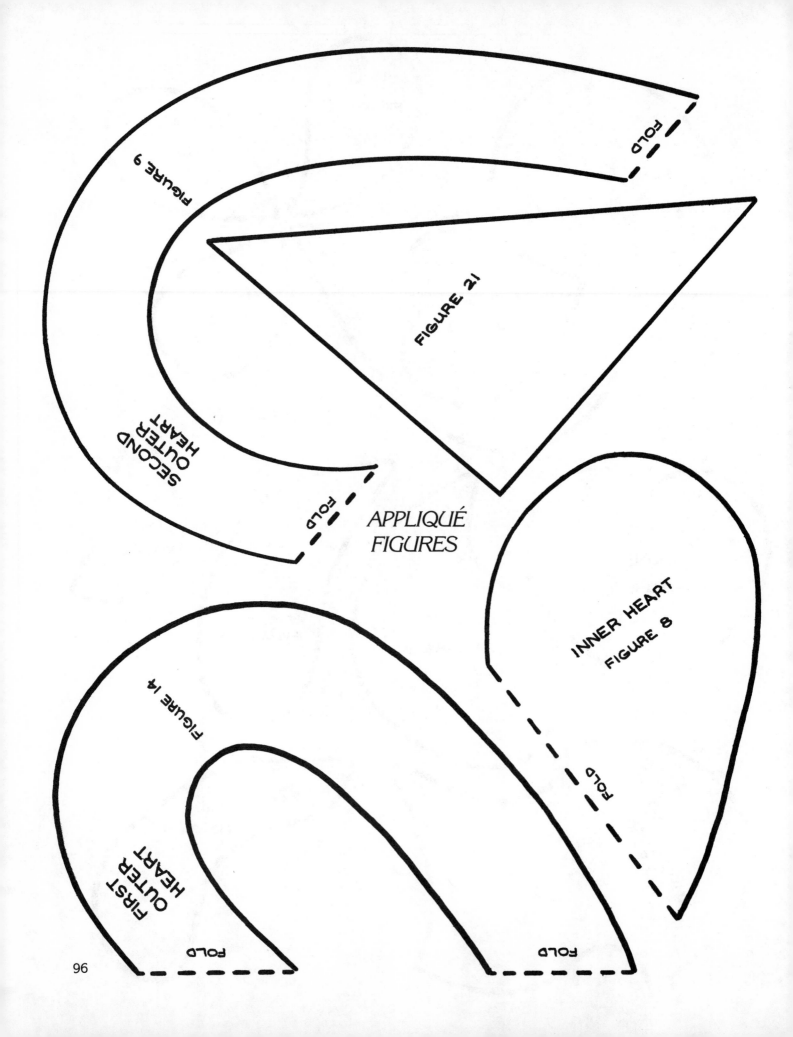

FIGURE 9

SECOND OUTER HEART

FOLD

FIGURE 21

APPLIQUÉ FIGURES

INNER HEART

FIGURE 8

FOLD

FIGURE 14

FIRST OUTER HEART

FOLD

FOLD

FOLD

96

PLACEMENT GUIDE
for Central Appliqué Motif

FIGURE 7

FIGURE 10

FIGURE 15

FIGURE 17

FIGURE 9

FIGURE 14

FIGURE 11

FIGURE 8

FIGURE 16

FIGURE 4

FIGURE 6

FIGURE 3

FIGURE 5

FIGURE 2

FIGURE 1

QUILTING DESIGNS

AILEEN STANNIS · *Berkley, Michigan*

CAKE STAND

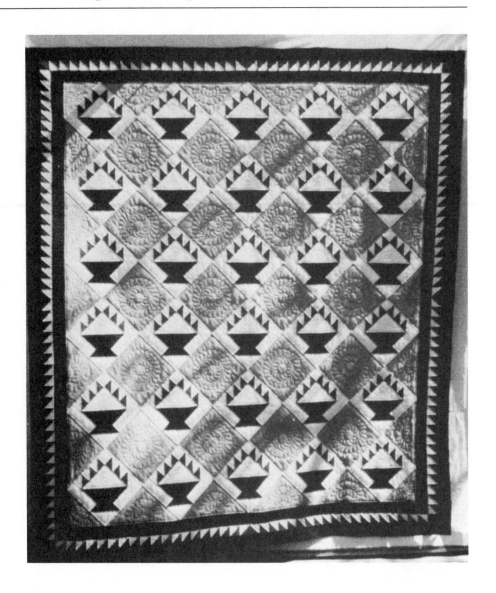

*U*sing just three fabric colors in the old-fashioned Cake Stand design, Aileen Stannis has produced a dramatic interpretation of a time-honored favorite. In her **Cake Stand,** *the simple geometric pattern of the design is countered by the swirls and delicacy of the intricate quilting.*

Aileen is one of those quilters who, until 1976, knew nothing about quilts. After she attended a quilt show, she was inspired to start quilting. She prefers traditional quilts and likes to reproduce antique quilts.

Her prizewinner **Cake Stand** *won First Prize Blue Ribbon at the Michigan State Fair as well as Best of Show Ribbon.*

"Accuracy in drafting a pattern, making the templates, and cutting the fabric pieces equals a good quilt," Aileen says.

"I try always to have one quilt in a frame for quilting, and one or two quilts in the process of piecing—thinking at the same time about the next one I will make."

MATERIALS

100 percent cotton fabrics, polyester batting, and a fine unbleached muslin for the backing.

CUTTING GUIDE

Cutting pieces and measurements do *not* include seam allowances. There are 30 pieced blocks in the quilt.

For each 10″ block, cut the following:

Figure A:	Figure C:	Figure D:
1 navy	6 red	1 muslin
1 muslin	6 muslin	Figure E:
Figure B:	2 navy	1 muslin
2 muslin		

From tiny-print navy-and-white fabric, cut:
  20 blocks 10″ square
  18 half-blocks
  4 quarter-blocks (for corners)
For navy print borders, cut 2 strips 2½″ × 90½″ and 2 strips 2½″ × 99½″
For 2″ sawtooth border, cut:
  Figure C:
    172 red
    172 muslin

ASSEMBLY

For each block, sew together 2 figure A triangles (1 navy and 1 muslin), along the long edge, to form a large square. Next join together pairs of the figure C triangles in red and muslin to form small squares. Attach the squares in 2 sets of 3 to the figure E corner muslin, forming an L. Then attach this unit to the muslin half of the large square.

Join the 2 figure B muslin rectangles to the 2 figure C navy print triangles. Join with the figure D muslin piece, forming an L. Then attach this unit to the dark navy A triangle.

Complete all 30 blocks in the same manner.

After completing the blocks lay out the entire quilt top on a table or floor, alternating pieced and plain fabric blocks, using the half- and quarter-blocks to square the borders. Then sew together in diagonal strips. Join these strips to form a complete quilt top.

Next add the first of the navy borders.

Piece and attach the sawtooth border. Complete the quilt top by adding the final navy border.

Attach to the muslin backing with the polyester batting in between.

Quilting is added to the plain blocks in a feathery design. In the pieced blocks, quilting is ¼″ around seam lines and fluted quilting is added to open areas. See Quilting Designs for placement. A ¼″ seam binding is used to complete the quilt.

Finished quilt is 85¾″ × 100″.

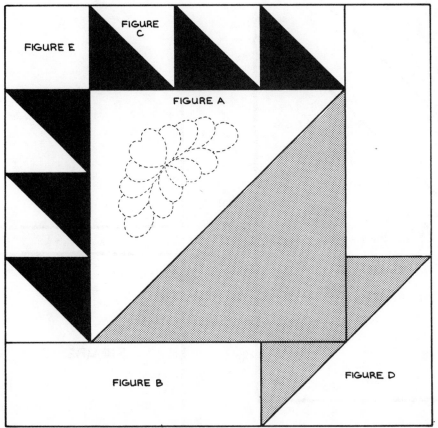

PIECING GUIDE

FIGURE E

FIGURE C

FIGURE A

FIGURE B

FIGURE D

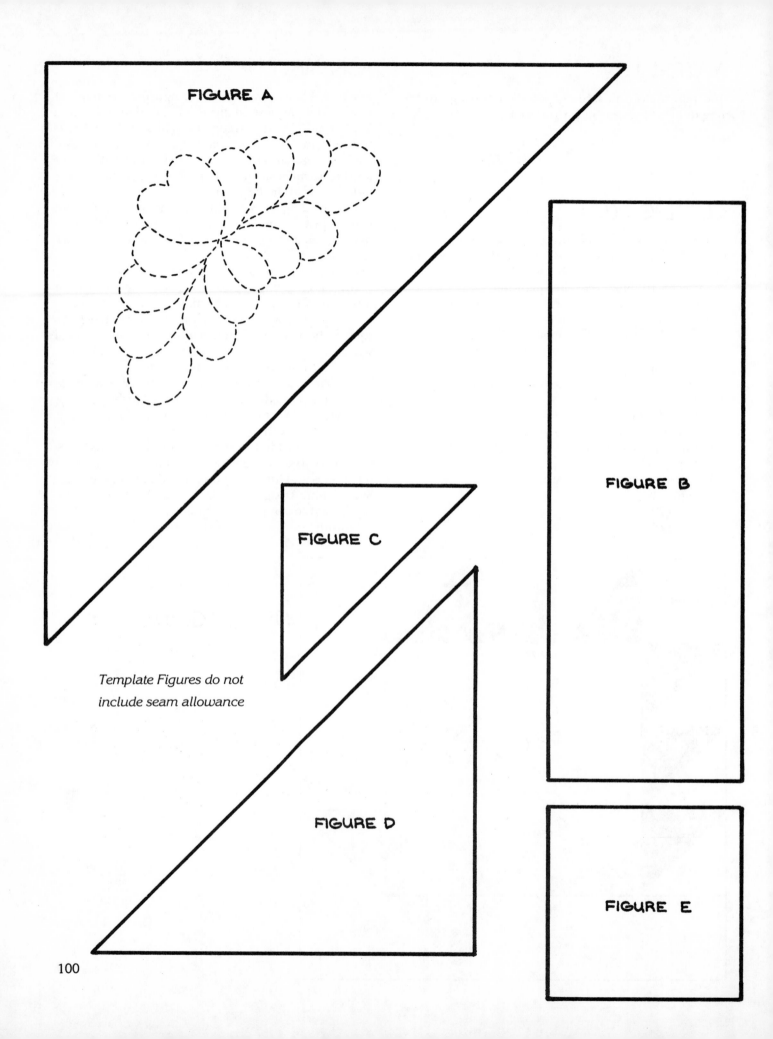

FIGURE A

FIGURE B

FIGURE C

Template Figures do not include seam allowance

FIGURE D

FIGURE E

100

QUILTING DESIGN

QUILTING DESIGN FOR PLAIN BLOCKS   101
(shown at 50 percent of full size; use the graph lines to enlarge to full size)

LILLIAN LINDGREN · *Chisago City, Minnesota*

FAN QUILT

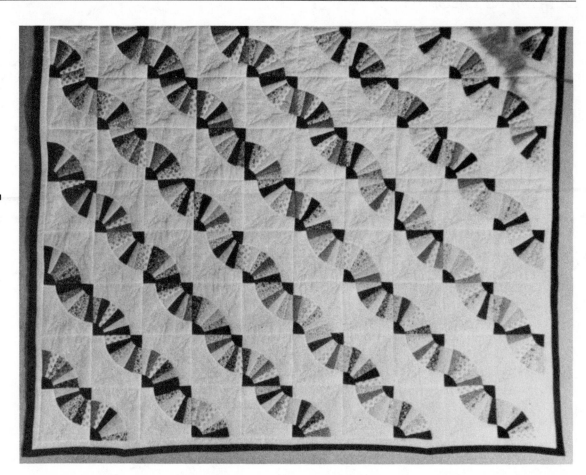

Miss Lillian Lindgren celebrated her ninetieth birthday in April 1983. Her Fan Quilt won a Blue Ribbon at the Minnesota State Fair. Miss Lindgren chose the pattern because "I liked the idea of reversing each square, making a path with the fans."

Her father was the only quilter in her family. "My father was a tailor in Sweden. When I was twenty-two years old, he and I made a quilt together. He did his own design and was very fussy and precise. He impressed upon me the importance of working with straight lines and even stitches. His influence apparently made a mark on how I do my work.

"Even though I am ninety years old and have cataracts, I love to keep busy sewing and quilting. I have sewed all my life. When I was eighteen years old, I worked in an exclusive dressmaker's shop in Duluth, Minnesota. The owner would often travel to Paris to get original designs and patterns. Then, I would sew 'Paris-design' dresses for the fashionable ladies in Duluth."

Miss Lindgren has been a long-time resident in the Margaret S. Parmly Nursing Home. A special thanks goes to Sally Rajamaki, the activities director, for arranging for the photographs and for sending the background information about this outstanding prizewinner.

MATERIALS

⅔ yard each of 6 assorted cotton prints for fan
6½ yards of dark brown cotton for backing
6½ yards of muslin or white cotton
½ yard of dark brown for center of fan

CUTTING GUIDE

There are eighty 10″ blocks in this quilt. Templates shown *include* ¼″ seam allowance. Border measurements do *not* include seam allowance.

For each block, cut:
    Figure A—1 dark brown fabric
    Figure B—6 from 6 different prints
    Figure C—1 from white or muslin fabric
    Two border strips–2″ × 80″ from muslin
    Two border strips–2″ × 98½″ from muslin

ASSEMBLY

Stitch the 6 figure B pieces to form fan. Next attach to this unit figure A to complete center of fan. To complete block sew figure C to the finished fan, as shown in Piecing Guide.

Stitch together all the blocks in the same manner. When all of the blocks are finished, arrange them on a table top or floor, reversing each square and making a path with the fans.

Next, add the muslin border.

After the top piecing has been completed, set the quilt into a frame, with the batting and backing.

Quilting is done with brown thread, stitching around each piece ¼″ from seam line. The plain muslin segment of each fan block is quilted with an abstract motif, shown in the Quilting Design.

After quilting has been completed, the brown backing is turned to the front and stitched down to form the final brown border.

The finished quilt measures 108″ by 88″.

PIECING AND QUILTING GUIDE

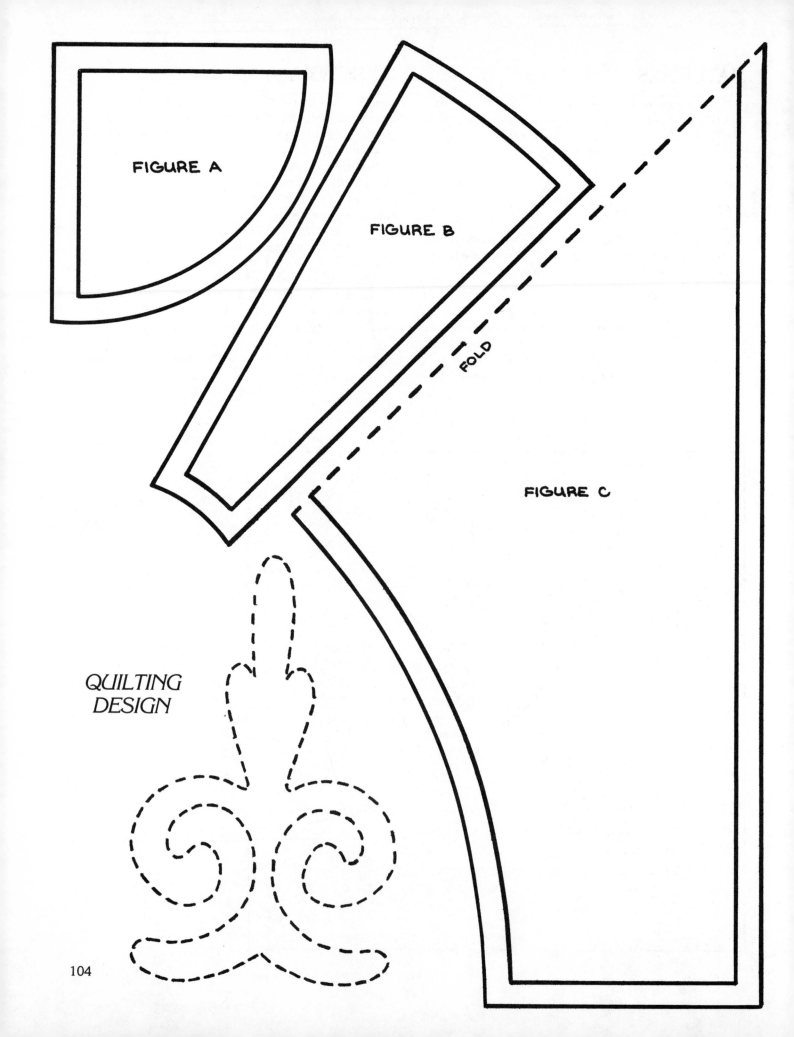

FIGURE A

FIGURE B

FOLD

FIGURE C

QUILTING
DESIGN

104

MISSISSIPPI WILD ROSE

*T*he regal design of this magnificently hand-appliquéd quilt is enhanced by the simple and appropriate choice of colors and shapes. Exquisite details are highlighted by the exceptional quilting and precision in drafting this design.

"I could talk quilts all day any day," Lillian Stubbs claims. "I breathe quilts." Her quilting has been of great help to her in dealing with both a family tragedy and recent illness. But putting her sorrow and sickness aside, Lillian aimed to complete six quilts last year and she made it.

"Most of my quilts I give away. I am making one now for my doctor as a gift. Quilting was a family tradition. I made my first blouse at the age of six and stood at the quilting frame when I quilted." She has been quilting for seventy-seven years.

Mississippi Wild Rose won a Blue Ribbon for Best in Its Class at the Mississippi State Fair and the tri-color for Best at the Fair. Mrs. Stubbs chose this pattern because "My mother made one similar to this when I was young and I loved it."

MATERIALS

10 yards of unbleached muslin for top and backing of quilt. Two yards each of red and green cotton prints for appliqué. Dacron batting.

CUTTING GUIDE

Figure templates do *not* include seam allowance.

Cut 9 muslin 22½″ squares (seam allowance included) for quilt top.

For center appliqué for each of 9 blocks, cut:

Figure 1–8 green print
Figure 2–8 red print
Figure 3–4 red print
Figure 4–24 green print
4 pieces of bias material 1½″ by 10½″ (seam allowance included). Fold in ¼″ on each side and baste.

For border appliqué, cut:

Figure 5–25 red print
Figure 6–25 green print

ASSEMBLY

For each block, draw a circle with tailor's chalk 17½″ in diameter, so that it is neatly centered on the square. Draw an X through the circle, beginning the lines at the corners of the square: This will give the point to place piece cut from figure 1.

Place figure 1 with large end toward corner and small end toward center of square with small end touching ¼″ below circle line. Baste in place after fastening figure 2 to V shape of figure 1.

Place figure 3 with center on circle for bias material to go under figure 3. Hold bias a little tight on side over circle mark. This will make circle.

Fasten bias material under figure 3 and over figure 1. After appliquéing of the block, place 6 pieces cut from figure 4 near bias material in desired positions and appliqué.

Follow the above instructions for the other 3 appliqué roses that make up the block. Complete all 9 blocks.

Join all 9 blocks. Then attach a plain white border to achieve the dimensions desired: cut 2 strips equal to the quilt's length and attach to the sides. Next cut 2 strips long enough to cover the newly added side borders and attach to the top and bottom. Arrange pieces cut from figures 5 and 6 to form the border motifs and appliqué in place. A bias binding is attached to finish.

The center of each block is quilted with a rosette (see p. 8). The overall quilting is done in a grid pattern.

The finished quilt measures 99″ × 90″.

APPLIQUÉ PLACEMENT GUIDE

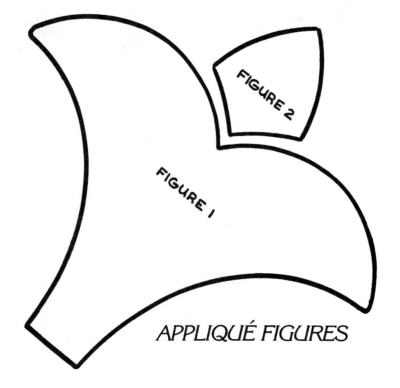

APPLIQUÉ FIGURES

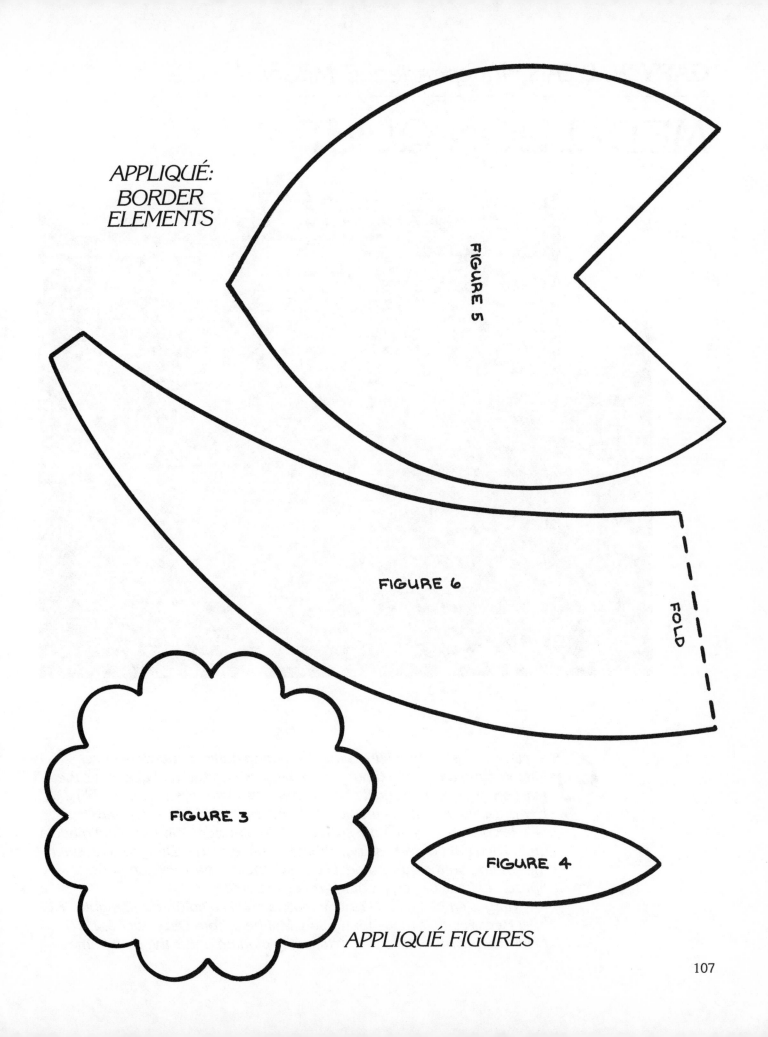

APPLIQUÉ:
BORDER
ELEMENTS

FIGURE 5

FIGURE 6

FOLD

FIGURE 3

FIGURE 4

APPLIQUÉ FIGURES

GARY W. DEAN · *Independence, Missouri*

MEDALLION QUILT

G ary Dean says, "When I first started showing quilts in Independence, Missouri, my wife and I would go to the show and stand back to get the reaction of the crowd. Most of the comments were, 'His wife probably did it.' After a few minutes, I would tell them I had made the quilt. Very few people could believe a man, six feet tall, two hundred pounds, had made a quilt. They would start asking: 'What is a backstitch?' 'Did you whipstitch the binding on the quilt?' and 'Let us see the needle pricks on your fingers.' I always enjoy proving I made the quilt."

Gary is employed by General Motors and is a volunteer firefighter. His quilt Medallion was made for his son, Matthew, born December 9, 1980. Matthew and his older sister, Kelli, enjoy playing under the quilt frame because it makes a great tent. "The most enjoyment in competition is making a quilt for someone special," Gary says, "and having it win a prize for them."

Gary's grandmother was a quilter, and he also took "quilt-as-you-go" classes. His suggestion to beginning quilters is, "If you start a quilt and find out you have to force yourself to work on it, start a different type of quilt or try working with different colors."

Though he has been quilting for several years, Gary started entering quilt competitions only in the last three years. Medallion won First Prize at the Missouri State Fair in 1981 and 1982.

Medallion quilts have a special place in the history of quiltmaking. They have long been a special tour de force force for the experienced quilter, and many have survived because they were so highly prized and therefore used as display or special-occasion quilts.

Precision is an absolute necessity if one is to attempt a medallion. Traditionally, there is a central panel or medallion, with carefully planned piecing around it, as in Gary Dean's example. This work, with the feel of a mosaic tile design, is based on a 1½-inch square and ¾" piecing. No fewer than eight major outer borders give unity to the central motif and the smaller borders framing that center.

The quilt top can be pieced in long horizontal strips or joined as each row is completed. Quilting is ¼" outside of the stitching lines of the light blue and navy blue fabric only, to give a textured and three-dimensional effect.

This quilt is quite adaptable and can be changed by using a smaller medallion center or by adding more borders. It can be entirely preplanned, but one of the delights of making this type of piece is that it need not be precisely worked out beforehand. After completion of the central medallion motif, borders can be added as time and whim dictate. There can be as many borders, of any width or pattern, as the quilter chooses.

Medallions are excellent quilt-as-you-go projects and they also make a fine choice for a family heirloom.

JEWELL WOLK · *Cut Bank, Montana*

WOMEN OF THE PLAINS

*T*his story-telling quilt was designed to give proper recognition to the Plains women and the role they played. This well-conceived artwork depicts significant scenes from the lives of these remarkable women.

Jewell Wolk lives on the edge of the Blackfoot Reservation in Cut Bank, Montana, and has known its inhabitants most of her life. In fact, in addition to their three children, the Wolks adopted four youngsters, including three Blackfoot daughters.

"My avocation is making story-telling quilts. This is my third one. My first honored the early-day schoolteachers—my mother was one. The second tells about the sheep industry before the days of the homesteaders.

"This one honors the Plains women. It has always been my feeling that the men were lauded far more than the women. So I set about honoring them."

Women of the Plains won First Place at the J. K. Ralston Museum Quilt Show.

"This quilt is a tribute to the women who nurtured a culture. Quilted into the sky is an eagle, which was considered a holy bird, a solar or sun bird. The eagle's feathers were regarded as rays from the sun. An earned feather was similar to our Medal of Valor."

These are some of the many aspects of the life of the Plains women that are represented in this quilt:

110

Breaking Her Pony. *Most children were good riders by the time they were five. Each young girl would be given a pony to train.*

Wood Gathering and Root Gathering. *This was a job only for women. The woman always took her digging stick and root pouch with her whenever she traveled any distance. Her stick, which was hardened over a slow-burning fire, was buried with her when she died.*

Wedding Party. *Weddings differed in all of the Plains tribes. The one shown is of the gens system, where the new bride goes to her husband's mother's lodge. (If it were the clan system, he would go to her lodge.)*

The girl is dressed in her finest white buckskin with blue porcupine beading on the sleeve. The blue beads are an indication of wealth. With her bridesmaid, the bride has encircled the half-mile campground, or three arrow flights from a good bow, and is preparing to dismount to her mother-in-law's back. She will get a piggyback ride into the lodge where her new bed and a feast are waiting.

Medicine Bundles. *The bundles could contain anything: roots, teeth, locks of hair, seeds, and almost always, buffalo stones. These were special mollusk fossils, neatly covered with buckskin, painted or beaded, with a small opening in the leather so the stone could look out. They were used to call the buffalo. There were many special kinds of bundles: love, hunting, tattooing, horse breeding, horse stealing, to name a few. Sacred bundles were often kept in medicine lodges where no women were allowed.*

Other depicted subjects include: Tanning a Hide; Buffalo Calf Wrestling; Courtship; Suicide; Mourning; Birth Defects; Blanket Courting; and Brotherly Encouragement.

HIGH SUMMERTIME

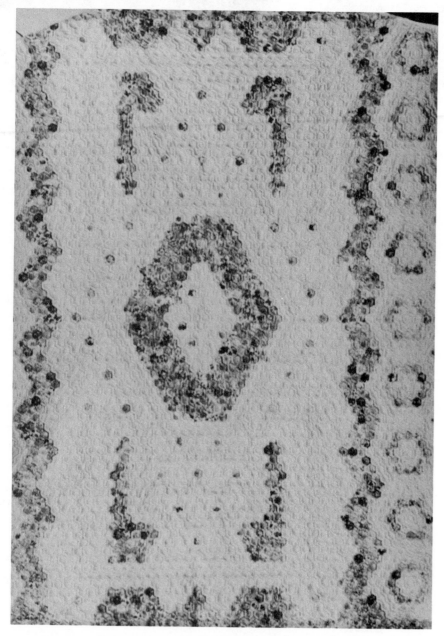

Mrs. Floy Buell, an eighty-three-year-old grandmother, made this special quilt for her son and daughter-in-law. High Summertime is just one of her many quilts that have won Blue Ribbons at the Nebraska State Fair.

About a year after she completed the quilt, the couple was killed in a tragic automobile accident, "so it has a special endearment for me."

This quilt has over five thousand pieces. "I measured my hexagon from another quilt I had made to get the size. Every printed hexagon has a suggestion of summer—flowers, birds, bees, et cetera. I then set them in the flower garden to make a queen-size quilt."

Mrs. Buell, who has been quilting more than fifty years, has these suggestions to pass along. "The most important thing is to learn to use a thimble. Also, make all the points 'hit' when piecing. In the quilting make the stitches fine and even, at least seven stitches to the inch, but eight or nine is better."

Mrs. Buell's mother learned fine sewing and tailoring as a young girl, and later used it as a means to support her family.

Mrs. Buell entered her first patchwork, a hand-pieced quilt top, in a quilt contest in 1906, when she was only five-and-a-half years old.

This quilt is composed entirely of hand-joined hexagons arranged in careful geometric shapes to give the illusion of a summer garden. To form each of the more than five thousand pieces Mrs. Buell suggests the following method:

For greatest accuracy, cut one paper hexagon for each fabric piece to be joined. Then, using a template that measures ¼ inch larger on each side than the paper hexagon, cut fabric hexagons from scraps of printed and plain cottons.

With paper hexagon centered on each fabric piece as a guideline, fold over the ¼ inch, one side at a time, and hand-baste through all three layers, including paper. Paper can be removed after basting, if desired. Repeat for each hexagon.

Press each piece after basting. Paper can be removed at any point up until the quilt top is attached to batting and backing.

Once the overall design is decided on, attach hexagons with small, even overstitching in desired pattern. When all hexagons are attached, join to backing and batting, and quilt entire quilt ¼ inch inside the seam allowances. Quilt can either be finished by squaring it off, or it can be left in the form of the motif of the quilt.

This is another quilt, like the Medallion Quilt on page 108, that lends itself beautifully to the quilt-as-you-go method; each hexagon can form a complete unit of top, batting, and backing. Also, like the medallion quilts, its finished dimensions may be dictated by the quilter's whims; additional rows of hexagons may be added until the quilt top has reached the desired size.

HAPPY "BIRTH" DAY BABY

*H*appy "Birth" Day Baby *quilt is Joyce Ganser's own design and she saw a similar pattern about twenty years ago. Since then she has perfected the design and written instructions for it.*

Over the years, she has made this quilt for "about twenty new babies in the family and for friends." It is all hand-quilted and hand-appliquéd and has won First Prize at the Nevada State Fair.

Joyce learned to quilt at church more than twenty-eight years ago, but it was a family tradition, as well. Her grandmother and mother were both quilters.

She doesn't enter competitions frequently now, since she is considered a professional and is no longer eligible to enter at the State Fair level. She has her own shop, and teaches and judges quilt competitions as well. Joyce has worked hard to promote the art of quilting in the state of Nevada. Her enthusiasm for her work is reflected in any conversation that leads to quilting.

She advises beginners to "take a class to learn the basic techniques before you learn bad habits."

The appliqué on this quilt is really very easy—the petals are cut as diagramed—one side is finger-pressed under and the other side is gathered. This gives the petal shape. It is then appliquéd in place by hand. It is a very old technique. Add a little embroidery, the self-ruffles, and the quilting, and it looks like the top of a birthday cake. Joyce generally uses white as the background, adding pink, yellow, and blue flowers with yellow and green centers. She also uses poly-cotton fabrics, so that the quilt can be washed and still look brand-new. Other colors can be used. This quilt can be made larger by adding another row of appliqué around the outside edge or by using the quilt as a medallion and adding borders. A pillow can also be made from the design.

CASTLE MAGIC

*T*his compelling composition is another example of the successful union of classic design with spectacular contemporary innovation. Each detail—delicate gull design of the border to all the geometric variations—adds to its appeal.

"After two generations I have revived the spirit of quilting," says Marguerite, "and others in my family have now begun to get the fever." Her great-grandmother, whose specialty was crazy quilts, had been the last in the family to quilt until Marguerite revived the art.

Marguerite's Castle Magic (© 1982) is her own design, named by her. "Designing a quilt on paper is much easier than translating that design into fabric. Therefore, I found this project most challenging and ultimately most rewarding when it was completed. I couldn't wait to begin my next challenge."

This winner has taken a Blue Ribbon at the Vermont Quilt Festival and First Place at the Franconia Quilt Show.

Marguerite feels that "It is most important to learn the basic skills of quilting. Once the foundation is laid, you can go from one phase up to the next one. It is a constant learning and sharing process. I hope I never stop learning."

She works in a variety of fabrics—cotton, cotton-blend, some wool, corduroy, and velveteen.

Castle Magic is an inventive and striking adaptation of a traditional patchwork block called Castle Wall. Its bold design creates a three-dimensional effect from the judicious placement of light and dark fabrics. To create Castle Magic Marguerite enlarged a single Castle Wall block to form a central medallion (with a delicate Rising Star at its very center, for added interest), then expanded this central figure with the addition of eight sweeping, two-colored rays that extend beyond the block's diamond-shaped border to define an octagonal frame. This large medallion is centered on a light-colored field, and bordered with the same handsome paisley print that is featured in the central figure.

Fine hand-quilting in linear geometric patterns echoes the quilt design by appearing to emanate from the point of each of the eight rays. The finished piece measures 55" × 55".

RICHARD F. ZIMMERMAN · *Bergenfield, New Jersey*

ROSE OF SHARON SAMPLER

*T*he Rose of Sharon Sampler, *which won First Prize at the Morristown, New Jersey, Quilt Show, was made as a result of a request by Richard Zimmerman's students for a quilt of flower appliqué.*

Richard is a self-taught quilter whose family has had no history of quilting. He is not only an outstanding quilter with many original designs to his credit, he also teaches, often four or more classes per week. This is in addition to his full schedule as a full-time elementary school teacher and a busy father.

One area of quiltmaking which has fascinated him and in which he has worked for several years is the revival of quilted liturgical vestments. Nowadays, there is a growing interest in designing and working in this area, but Richard was challenged by these projects before the renewed popularity.

In many ways, he is a traditional quilter because he likes classic patterns and because he rarely goes out to buy everything for a quilt. He draws upon materials available at home and then purchases additional supplies as needed.

His advice to students and beginners is, "Read all you can about quilts and quilting, subscribe to periodicals on quilting, and **Practice, Practice, Practice."**

Richard Zimmerman shared his approach to perfect appliqué, which he used in his prizewinning flowered sampler: "Many quilters are familiar with the 'English' piecing technique. Pieces of fabric are basted over individual paper patterns, most often hexagons, then whipstitched together along the common edges. It is an ancient and time-honored approach to piecing. But what about using this same method (basting over paper shapes) for maintaining the exact shape of the appliqué pieces? Several years ago I began to use this approach for appliqué."

Trace the shapes of the individual pieces to be appliquéd onto a medium-weight paper. (Richard prefers to use white drawing paper which is strong enough to hold the fabric in shape, yet light enough to cut easily.) When the design calls for multiple units of the same size and shape, trace the shape only once for every four needed. Staple four thicknesses of paper to the drawing, and cut out four shapes at one time.

Next, place the paper patterns face down on the back of the fabric, pin to secure in place, and cut out fabric, adding ¼-inch seam allowance.

Baste the seam allowances over the edges of the paper patterns.

On the background fabric, mark the total design to be appliquéd, using a chalk pencil or "wash-out" fabric-marking pen, but not a regular lead pencil. This is your master plan for the placement of the various parts. Once the appliqué is complete, the master plan can be washed out, leaving only the appliquéd design on a clean background.

Place the first shape to be appliquéd in position according to the plan marked on the background fabric. Pin and appliqué using a blind or slip stitch, or whatever stitch you usually use. (Be careful to catch only the edge of the fabric shape—not the paper pattern.)

As each shape is appliquéd, remove pins. Turn the work over. With the point of a small scissors, cut into the back of the background fabric behind the appliqué. (The paper liner will prevent cutting the newly appliquéd fabric.) Cut away the background fabric to within ¼-inch of appliqué stitches. Remove basting stitches and paper liner.

Place next set of shapes to be appliquéd and proceed as above. Continue until all shapes have been appliquéd, and design is complete. Remove markings of master design by washing.

This method assures smooth curves; sharp points, both inside and outside; straight edges; and exact duplication of the original design.

FLOWER SAMPLER

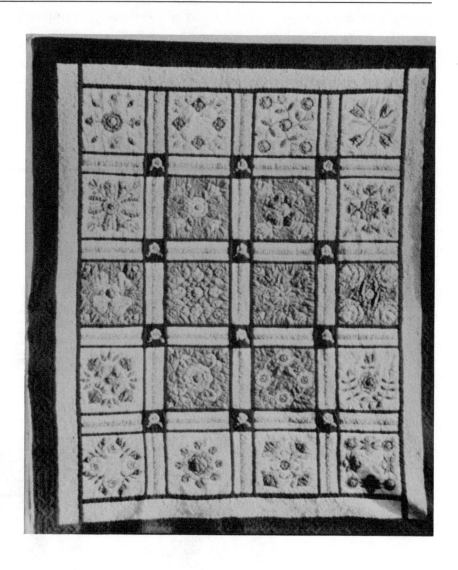

*T*his grand flower-lover's quilt is composed of twenty classic appliqué patterns, using contemporary colors of light pink, turquoise, and rose. The well-designed borders and the intricate quilting complete this original sampler variation.

Until three and a half years ago, Carol Meyer had never even seen a quilt, let alone made one. While vacationing in Kentucky, she went to a quilt show and was so enthusiastic about learning that immediately upon her return home she signed up for classes.

In September 1982, she entered two quilts in competition at the New Mexico State Fair, and although she had "never won anything" before, came away with First Prize in two categories. Her Flower Sampler won First Place in the appliqué-quilt category and another quilt, her Indian Life quilt, won First Place in the pieced-quilt category.

Carol, like many other quilters, has an active family (four children and a policeman husband) to care for, but she finds the quiet hours at night, while her husband is working, a good time to quilt.

Her advice to new quilters is, "Don't be afraid to try something new or different."

MATERIALS

For the background blocks and the borders, you will need cottons and cotton blends in the following colors:

    Color A: light pink cotton
    Color B: medium rose cotton
    Color C: deep rose
    Color D: light print for lattice work

CUTTING GUIDE

The following measurements are for the background blocks and borders. Measurements do *not* include seam allowances.

    20 blocks, 15″ square: 12 in color A, 8 in color B
    2 borders 5″ × 78″ in color A
    2 borders 5″ × 108″ in color A
    2 borders 7″ × 102″ in color C
    2 borders 7″ × 122″ in color C
    Twelve 6″ squares in color C
    2 strips 1½″ × 78″ in color C
    2 strips 1½″ × 108″ in color C
    155 strips 1½″ × 15″: 62 in color A, 62 in color C, 31 in color D

ASSEMBLY

Each of the 20 blocks in Carol's quilt represents a different, traditional floral appliqué design from various sources.

1. California Rose
2. Hollyhock Wreath
3. Whig Rose
4. Tulip (crib)
5. Tulip design
6. Rose and Tulip
7. Texas Rose
8. Rose of Sharon
9. Ohio Rose
10. Iowa Rose
11. Currants & Cockscombs
12. Tulip
13. Lancaster Rose
14. New Jersey Rose
15. North Carolina Rose
16. Prairie Rose
17. Rose Wreath
18. Washington Rose
19. Indiana Rose
20. President's Wreath

Choose the floral designs you wish to use, and appliqué on the 15″ blocks.

When all 20 blocks have been appliquéd, they are arranged according to the Piecing Diagram, with the dark blocks forming a cross surrounded by the light pink blocks.

To assemble quilt top, connect the blocks by pieced latticework strips and small appliquéd squares. Each lattice section consists of five 15″ strips pieced according to color: C, A, D, A, C. Join 4 appliquéd blocks with pieced lattice sections to form a horizontal row. Repeat with remaining appliqué blocks, forming 5 rows of 4 blocks. Next, join 4 lattice segments, alternating with small appliquéd squares in a long strip. Once all remaining lattice segments and small squares have been stitched together, assemble quilt top, alternating rows of appliquéd blocks with long lattice-and-square strips.

To finish, attach the dark rose 1½″ × 78″ borders to the top and bottom edges of the quilt, and follow with the 5″ × 78″ pink borders along the top and bottom. Then attach the 1½″ × 108″ borders to each side (including the new border just added) followed by the 5″ × 108″ borders. Last, the 7″ borders are added, first to top and bottom, then to sides. Bias binding in pink is the finishing touch.

The quilting for each appliquéd block is slightly different, according to the appliqué designs themselves. For the latticework (light segments only) and the 5″ border, Quilting Design Border 1 is used; Quilting Design Border 2 is used for the wide outer border.

The finished quilt measures 102″ × 122″.

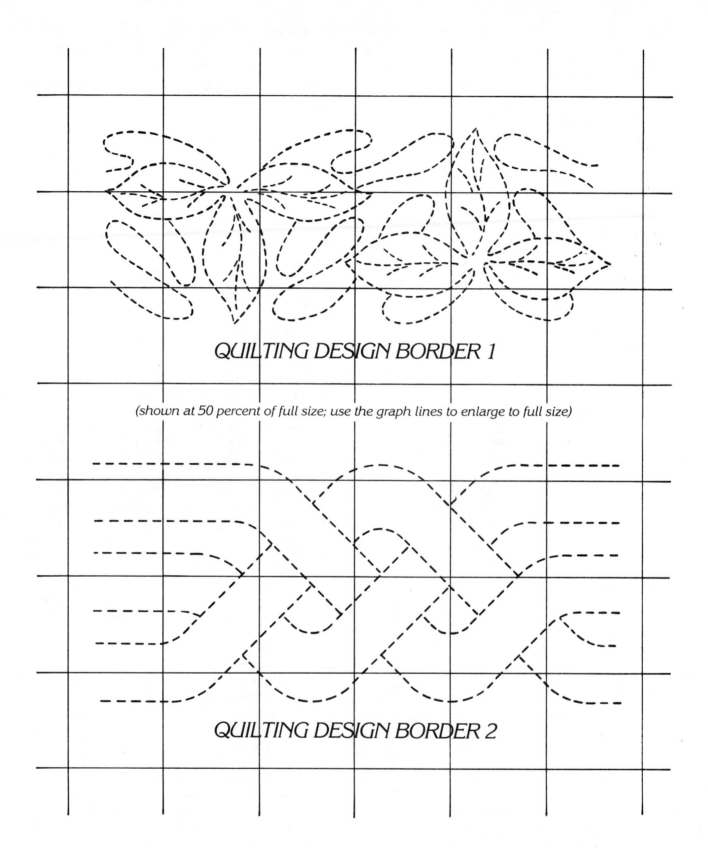

QUILTING DESIGN BORDER 1

(shown at 50 percent of full size; use the graph lines to enlarge to full size)

QUILTING DESIGN BORDER 2

JEAN LINDEN AND THE STUDENTS OF P.S. 48
Jamaica, Queens, New York

INTERNATIONAL YEAR OF THE CHILD

"*Everything is fair in love, war, and getting children to read,*" claims Jean
Linden. That is how she came to start her "Read It and Quilt It" project.
"Television-age children are, in many cases, less book-oriented than
children of earlier years. Our first quilt began as a banner contest to cele-
brate Library Media Day in New York State. Each child was to read a book
and then make a picture in felt of the main character. The pictures turned
out so well that we mounted them on calico squares and put them
together in a quilt. It won a blue ribbon in the children's section of the
Brooklyn Needlework Show. The children who made it appeared on
educational television and at educational meetings at colleges. That beginning effort led to more projects, including a Bicentennial quilt centered on
Benjamin Franklin.*"

For International Year of the Child, *Mrs. Linden began a project with*

*fourteen sixth-grade boys and girls working during any time available—
lunch hours, recesses, and so forth. The students used an atlas to make a
map of the world and marked each area or country to be represented by a
child in the quilt. "For areas not among our patterns, we researched
costumes of these missing countries and added six patterns of our own."*

*The resulting quilt was chosen to be hung in the office of the Secre-
tary of Education in Washington, D.C. The class was invited to Washington for the opening and to give a quilting demonstration.*

*Mrs. Linden and her classes have produced nearly twenty quilts,
which hang at the school. "I'll do anything to get them to read," said Mrs.
Linden; her quilts are proof that she has succeeded.*

MATERIALS

Felt, and scraps of fabrics in cotton, poly-cotton, et
cetera. (These materials are used when working with
large numbers of children having varying degrees of
sewing ability. All-cotton and more traditional fabrics
can be easily substituted.)

CUTTING GUIDE

Measurements are provided for background blocks
and borders. Seam allowances are *not* included.

> 20 blocks 8½" × 11" of felt
> 40 strips 8" × 2" in assorted printed fabrics, for
> latticework
> 40 strips 12" × 2" in assorted printed fabrics, for
> latticework
> 2 border strips 4" × 50"
> 2 border strips 4" × 60"

ASSEMBLY

Figures wearing international costumes are appliquéd onto the felt blocks:

Using scraps of fabric, assemble the costumed
figures and stitch all details in place. (The figures can
be cut out separately or drawn directly on the block.)

Next, border each felt block in print fabric, for a
finished block measuring 12" × 14½".

One completed block should be attached to the
next one, thus making strips. The 4 strips of 5 blocks
can then be joined.

Finally, add the border strips to complete the quilt
top. Attach batting and the backing, and the piece is
ready for quilting. It can be hand-quilted or tied in
any design the quilter chooses.

The finished quilt is 58" × 60".

Note: The felt blocks used in this piece measure
8½" × 11" (the size of a standard piece of typewriter
paper) so that the hand-drawn designs could be easily
translated into applique work without enlarging or
reducing the patterns.

MILDRED PATTERSON · *Raleigh, North Carolina*

HOME 1915–1925

*M*ade entirely by hand by Mildred Patterson, Home 1915–1925 *was Mildred's birthday gift to her older sister to recall their childhood days. It went on to win a Blue Ribbon in the North Carolina Quilt Symposium. Featured in this delightful collection of memories is the Briscoe family car, from which the steering wheel once came off in Mildred's father's*

hands as he was driving it; Frank, the gray horse who would not trot or run when older children held a baby on his back; the jars of fruit and vegetables which all family members helped to put up every summer; and the combined careers of Mildred's father—lawyer and farmer.

Mildred's quilt is unique because it incorporates the background quilting design she devised, which she calls her "chicken-track stitch." She won an award for this stitch at the Mordecai Needlework Show in Raleigh.

Her advice to other quilters is, "Keep trying . . . learn from others and enjoy quilting."

The design for this quilt is original, using representations of objects from Mildred's childhood arranged in "frames" around the home, which forms a central medallion.

The twenty-five blocks are of different sizes and shapes, depending upon their placement in the quilt and the particular design of each one. The scenes are joined with a binding of printed fabric. Much of the detail in these "pictures" is appliqué made from patterned fabric reminiscent of the years portrayed in the quilt. The "chicken-track stitch" is a continuous line of zigzag stitching which varies in size depending upon the needs of the particular object depicted in the frame.

SHIRLEY C. MUHLHAUSER · *Beulah, North Dakota*

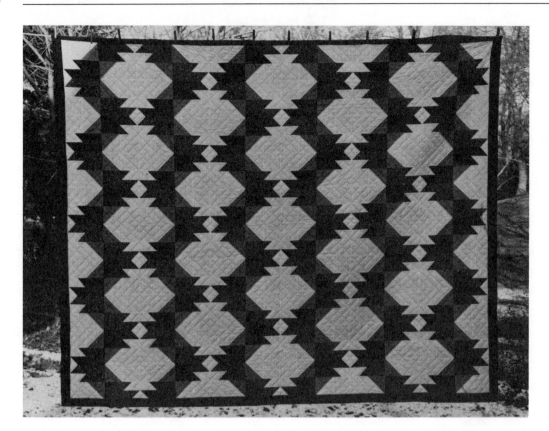

THE CHIEF

*T*his vibrant geometric pattern of red, black, white, and gray recalls dramatically classic Native American blanket designs. Yet its simple, clean, and precise effect is startlingly contemporary. This authoritative work joins the best of the past with the present, while joining two cultures through textile artistry.

Shirley Muhlhauser's quilting advice to her daughter was, "Be adventurous and try anything." And "Be precise." Her marvelous quilts are a reflection of that philosophy.

The Chief *was Grand Champion, Best of Show in the pieced and hand-quilted category at the Indian Summer Quilt Show and won First Prize at the North Dakota State Fair.*

Sadly, Mrs. Muhlhauser died in December 1982 before the completion of this book. However, through the help of her daughter, Tara Lea Muhlhauser, we have been able to learn of her mother's artistry as a quilter.

Shirley Muhlhauser preferred working with cotton scraps and rarely bought new fabric for quilting projects. The fabric for The Chief *came from dresses she had made for her daughters in the 1950s and 1960s. In addition to quilting, she sewed all of her daughters' clothing. Tara remembers, "I was in college before I had my first 'store bought' coat.*

"I feel very fortunate, as do my sisters, that some of her many talents were shared and will pass on to future generations."

MATERIALS

For a traditional American Indian blanket design, red, black, white, and gray cotton fabrics are used. Changing the color combination will achieve different effects; many variations are possible, depending upon the choices made by the quilter. Scraps of old cotton dresses were used. Dacron batting.

CUTTING GUIDE

Using the patterns shown below, cut patches in appropriate colors. Seam allowances are *not* included.

> Figure 1—60 red, 60 black
> Figure 2—60 red, 60 black
> Figure 3—20 white (for use in half- and quarter-blocks)
> Figure 4—230 white
> Figure 5—410 white, 120 tan
> Borders are bias strips in black.

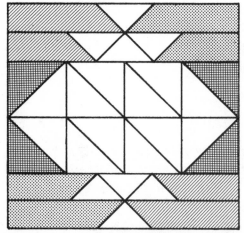

ASSEMBLY

The quilt consists of:
> 23 full blocks
> 4 blocks bisected, horizontally
> 8 blocks bisected, vertically
> 4 quarter-blocks

Begin by assembling full blocks according to Piecing Guide. Do the same for the vertical and horizontal half-blocks and the quarter-blocks.

To form quilt top, attach 5 full blocks in strips, pedestal end to pedestal end. This will form a small diamond between each pair of them.

Next join 4 full blocks in the same manner, with a horizontal half-block on each end. Join this strip to the first strip. Repeat, alternating 5-block and 4-block strips until all blocks are used. To finish, make 2 strips, each consisting of 4 vertical half-blocks with a quarter-block at each end, and join to top and bottom of quilt top.

To finish quilt top, attach the black border.

Quilting is according to stitching pattern in long diagonal rows of stitches.

The finished quilt is 72″ × 90″.

PIECING GUIDE

Detail of Quilting

Calendulas by Donna Eddy Andrew, page 134. (PHOTO BY DAVID JAMES OF EUGENE, OREGON)

Rose of Sharon Sampler by Richard F. Zimmerman, page 118. (PHOTO BY LYNNE AIKMAN)

Hearts & Flowers by Ernestine Costas, page 132. (PHOTO BY KATHY WARD)

Baltimore Friendship Quilt by Dorothy Sayre, page 130. (PHOTO BY CUBBERLY STUDIOS, INC.)

Happy "Birth" Cay Baby by Joyce Ganser, page 114. (PHOTO BY JOYCE V. GANSER)

The Chief by Shirley C. Muhlhauser, page 127. (PHOTO BY JAMES T. BRENNAN)

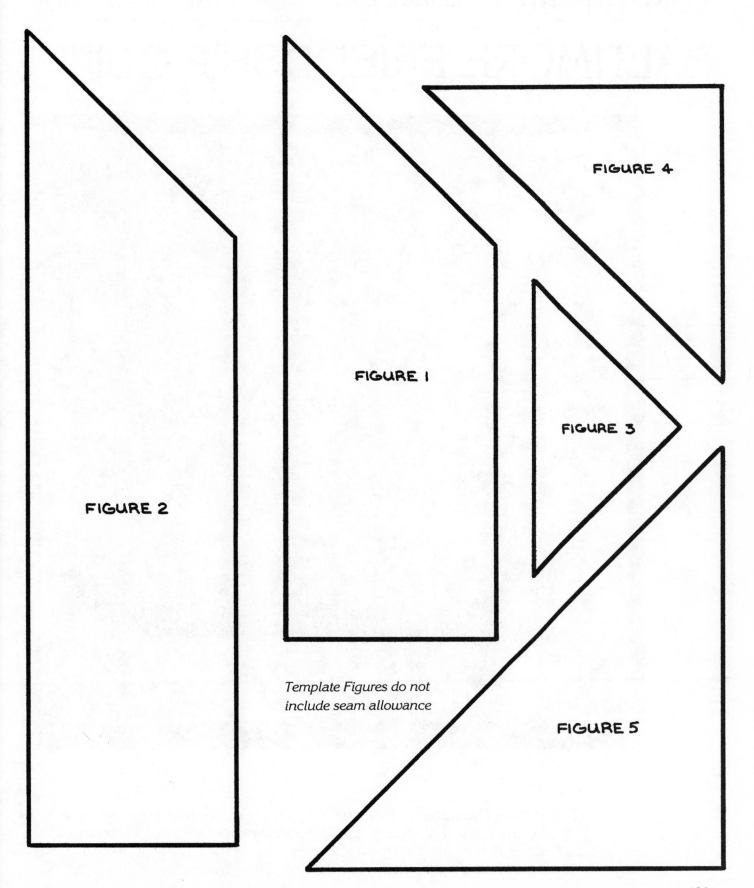

FIGURE 4

FIGURE 1

FIGURE 2

FIGURE 3

*Template Figures do not
include seam allowance*

FIGURE 5

DOROTHY SAYRE · *Hilliard, Ohio*

BALTIMORE FRIENDSHIP QUILT

*B*altimore Friendship quilts, of which this is such an excellent example, are the finest of album-style quilts. This exceptional piece incorporates many details that all work well together. Each one of the distinctive floral blocks is a complete unit that can stand alone. The rich selection of colors for

130

each detail, placed against a simple background, pull together to give an exceptional rendering of a classic American quilt.

During the 1982 Ohio State Fair, Dorothy Sayre exhibited her Baltimore Friendship Quilt *at the Fair's quilt show. Attendance at that particular exhibit was seventeen thousand, and this quilt was voted the favorite. It has also won Best of Show, Ohio State Fair; Best of Show, Franklin County Show; Best of Show, National Needlework Guild; and prizes at the Canadian Exposition and Woodlawn Plantation Show.*

Mrs. Sayre, who learned to quilt from an aunt, "by trial and error," has a history of quilting in her family. Her maternal grandmother, mother, and three aunts, all native West Virginians, were accomplished quilters.

"This quilt is copied from one owned by The Ladies of Mt. Vernon, Virginia. The original is on loan to the Museum of Modern Art in New York City. I enlarged patterns and transferred them to fabric. I then proceeded to make patterns of each small flower, bird, et cetera, and to choose the colors for each block. It took me six years to complete. (Whenever I thought that I was getting bored and might do a less than perfect job, I stored the blocks away for a while.) After completion of the top, my husband helped me mark the diamond quilting pattern on the top. This took several days. Then I quilted in the evenings for three months. I am a schoolteacher; therefore, all my needlework is done in the evenings."

To beginners she suggests, "Start with an easy pattern and be patient; start with blocks so that you'll be encouraged as each block is finished."

HEARTS & FLOWERS

*I*nspiration for Ernestine Costas' quilts comes from many sources; her romantic Hearts & Flowers *is a result of a valentine that her daughter sent her. The bouquet of flowers in red, blue, white, and shades of pink appliquéd on the tiny-print central heart gives a Victorian feeling to the quilt. The dark blue borders alternating with contrasting small-print borders make a perfect frame for the soft blue background of the piece.*

Hearts & Flowers won First Place in appliqué at the Oklahoma State Fair. All of Ernestine's quilts are made entirely by hand, and she has collected numerous awards for her efforts. Another of her blue ribbon prizewinners is Baseball Quilt, *made for her son, a Houston Astros' fan.*

Ernestine's advice to beginning quilters is to select a simple pattern and make just one block to begin with. If the block is successful and the quilter wishes, the quilt can be continued. If, however, the quilter decides that it isn't worth the effort of a large piece, the block can always be used for a pillow. Ernestine uses sandpaper to cut out pieces, because it keeps the fabric from slipping.

"Making a quilt is not easy; it is a hard job. But when you sew that last block, put it together, and bind the edge, it is so rewarding. I feel I have really accomplished a big job."

Ernestine uses different materials for different applications, but usually likes to work in 100 percent cotton and occasionally cotton-polyester. For this quilt, Ernestine cut out the heart center and the flowers and leaves freehand. She experimented with the flower arrangement and placement of the leaves until she felt it looked right, then appliquéd the flowers onto the heart. Next she appliquéd the heart onto the central blue background. Ernestine added a border at a time, and when she wasn't pleased with the effect, she took off the border and replaced it.

After all the borders were finished she scalloped the edges of the last border, completing the top. The back of the quilt uses the same light blue fabric of the central panel, and in the final step in assembly she bound the top, batting, and backing together.

The quilting followed the outline of the heart, and then a different quilt design was used to work a pattern out from the center to the borders, which also have various quilting motifs worked into them. Ernestine said that it took six to eight months to complete this project, "but a lot of that time was spent 'looking at the quilt'—looking to see what should be added next, which colors were the most pleasing, and so forth."

Detail of Quilting

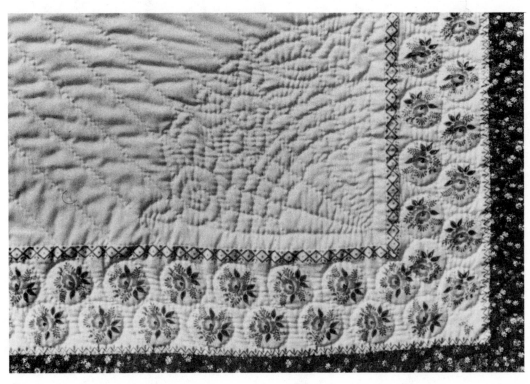

CALENDULAS

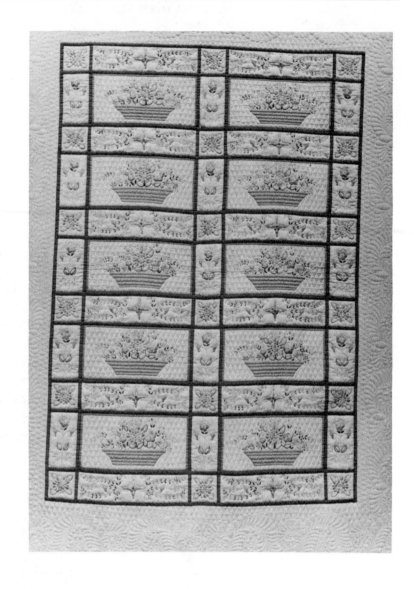

A t last count, **Calendulas,** *based on an original design that Donna Eddy Andrew adapted from a favorite note card, had collected at least a dozen top awards across the country. At the 1983 Santa Rosa Quilt Show this took the Best of Show award, First Prize in embroidery, as well as First Prize in its division, which includes six classes of quilts. It has won First Place and Best of Show at the Oregon State Fair; First Place and Best of Show at the 1981 National Quilt Association Show in Virginia; and other prizes in shows throughout the country.*

Calendulas took two years to make. Donna kept track of the time for the "quilting only." It totaled eight hours a day, seven days a week for six months. She used 1,154 yards of #40 cotton thread dipped in melted paraffin for added strength.

Donna started quilting twelve years ago. "In those days I spent a lot of time in the car waiting for one or the other of our five children who were busy with their varied activities. With all that idle time on my hands, quilting seemed to be the most natural thing to do."

But Donna had seen only one friend work on quilting blocks, and she had to find someone to show her what to do. She says, "I got the bug before I had even taken the first stitch." Her determination led her to ask questions and seek out the best quilter she could find. Her very first quilt won a Blue Ribbon at the county fair.

Quilting and the many friends she has made in her quilt club were a source of support when she was seriously ill and hospitalized. Encouragement from her family is also an important part of Donna's quilting, and she says that her husband, Paul, "must be used to my eating, drinking, and sleeping quilts. I took a few days off, and he said, 'You better get started on your next one.'"

MATERIALS

10 yards of drip-dry unbleached muslin for piecing and backing
2½ yards each of green and gold cotton fabrics for designs and borders
Polyester batting

CUTTING GUIDE

The following measurements are for backgrounds and borders. Measurements do *not* include seam allowances. *Read instructions before cutting.*

Unbleached muslin:
    10 rectangles 13″ × 6½″
    12 rectangles 13½″ × 3½″
    15 rectangles 7″ × 3½″
    Eighteen 3½″ squares
Green:
    12 strips 14″ × ½″
    3 strips 7″ × ½″
    6 strips 3½″ × ½″
    72 pieces ½″ × ½″
Gold:
    20 strips 15″ × ¼″
    20 strips 8″ × ¼″
Muslin:
    2 strips 10″ × 97″, 2 strips 10″ × 79″, for first border
    1 strip 9″ × 97″, 1 strip 9″ × 79″, for second border
Green:
    1 strip 62″ × ½″, 1 strip 80¼″ × ½″, for border
Gold:
    1 strip 62″ × ¼″, 1 strip 80″ × ¼″, for border

ASSEMBLY

Transfer embroidery designs to base fabric and finish embroidery before cutting out squares and rectangles, as it is hard to secure small pieces in an embroidery hoop. The flowers are embroidered with gold variegated floss, the leaves with variegated green, both in satin stitch. The basket was appliquéd in strips. One solid piece could be used, however, and the lines quilted for texture.

Frame the large embroidered rectangles with the ¼″ gold strips. Total measurement will then be 13½″ × 7″.

Then frame the blocks with the ½″ wide green fabric.

Using ½″ lattice strips, frame all blocks by horizontal rows, using the ½″ squares to complete them. Refer to photograph for placement. Complete and join all remaining rows. The quilt top now measures 40½″ × 62.″

After all the blocks are joined and completely framed with ½″ green strips, add the first 10″ muslin border. Again, frame with the green, then the gold, and add the second 10″ muslin border.

The intricate quilting follows the lines of the embroidery and appliquéd work, giving a trapunto effect. The borders are quilted with a feathery design (see the Quilting Design), and then the entire quilt is, stitched in a crosshatch pattern.

Mrs. Andrew used green for the binding because she felt it gave a better balance than the unbleached muslin would have.

The finished quilt measures 80″ × 102″.

These instructions use the greens and golds that Mrs. Andrew used. However, the quilter may choose any other color combination.

Appliquéd and Embroidered Block

Back of **Calendulas**

APPLIQUE AND EMBROIDERY DESIGNS

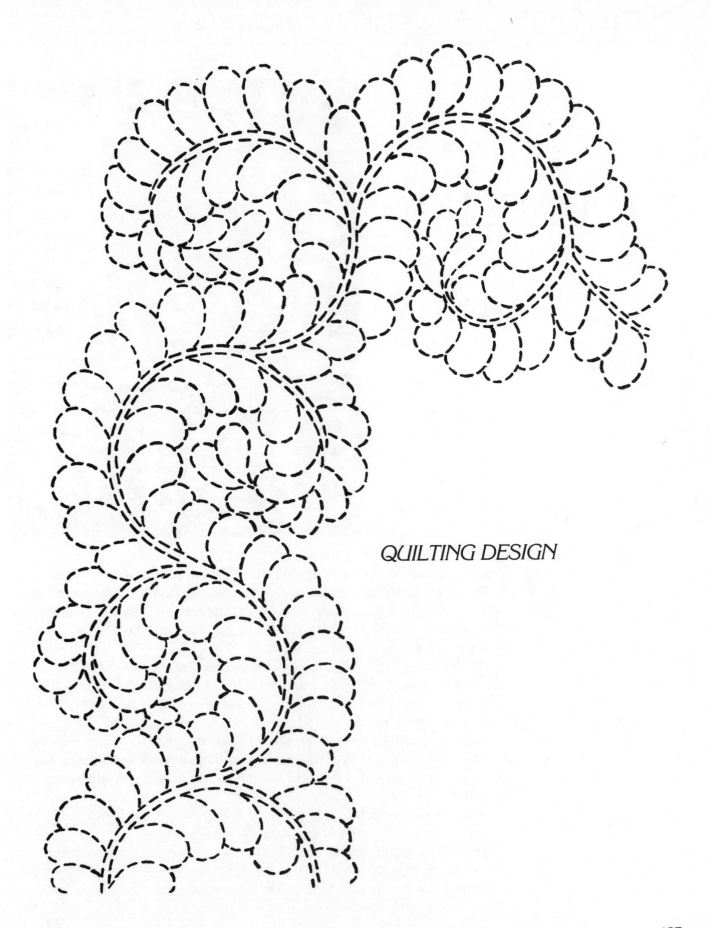

QUILTING DESIGN

3-D DAHLIA

*I*t is not unusual for Bertha Rush to be sought out for her advice on a quilting point. Even quilters twice her age call on Bertha for answers to their more perplexing questions. Judging from the exceptional quilting and pattern work in her prizewinning 3-D Dahlia, her reputation is well deserved in the quilting community.

Bertha has made numerous quilts, usually for the benefit of the Mennonite Church, of which she is a member. Her quilt 3-D Dahlia won First Prize and Special Award Ribbon at the Allentown Fair, and is one of Bertha's favorite designs.

Bertha started quilting when she was twelve years old. She learned from her mother, but can remember her grandmother piecing quilts as a regular hobby and recalls hearing pointers that her grandmother gave to her friends.

Bertha's advice to beginners is, "Do not be discouraged by your first attempt: quilting takes practice; your stitch will improve."

3-D Dahlia is simple in design but time-consuming because of the eight gathered petals around the center. Gathering the petals and keeping the center piece round are the challenges of this pattern. You can interchange colors in this pattern for a variety of effects.

MATERIALS

Cottons: White for background and parts of side panels; white-and-red print and solid red for flowers; dark red for side panels.

CUTTING GUIDE

Templates and measurements *include* ¼" seam allowance.

    For each of the fifteen 14" square blocks, cut:
        Figure 1–8 white-and-red print
        Figure 2–4 white
        Figure 3–4 white
        Figure 4–8 red
        Figure 5–1 white-and-red print
        Figure 6–24 red
        Figure 7–56 white
        38 strips of white fabric 14½" × 3½" for latticework
    For side panels, cut:
        40 dark red triangles, 20" long on each side and 6" wide at bottom. Measure the bottom straight (6"), but curve bottom when marking and cutting.
        38 white triangles the same size as the red, except without the curve.
        4 additional white triangles slightly larger than the above for the corners. The size will differ according to the bed size—measure carefully before cutting.

ASSEMBLY

Clip along the curves of the wedge cut from figure 1.

Join the 4 triangles cut from figure 2 to the right, straight sides of 4 wedges cut from figure 1, making certain the long side of the triangle is to the left of the unjoined side of the triangle. Spread flat.

Seam the 4 squares cut from figure 3 to the right, straight sides of the other 4 wedges cut from figure 1. Spread flat.

Sew a "petal" cut from figure 4 to the left curve of each wedge-triangle unit and each wedge-square unit. Follow the directional arrows of the figures, and stretch the wedge curve to fit the petal curve. The petal will be on the bottom as you sew.

Alternately sew the petal-wedge-triangle units to the petal-wedge-square units, until the outside edges of the block are joined. Sew each seam from the outside edge of the block toward the inside curved edge with a petal on the bottom, stretching the wedge curve to fit the petal curve. "Butt" seams at the point of the petal so that the petal seam allowance is pinned away from the petal.

Note. Butting seams: When preparing to sew horizontal rows together in a long seam, fit the rows right sides together and fold back the top edges of the seam allowance, so you can see the vertical seam joints on the inside. *Butt* these joints against each other perfectly. Finger press or pin the vertical seam allowance on the joint of one row in one direction, and the seam allowance of the matching joint of the other row in the opposite direction.

A correctly "butted" seam joint will fall flat, without ridges or bumps.

If pins are used, pin through each seam allowance, not through the seam joint itself. Do this across the row as often as necessary.

For perfectly matched joints, it is more important to have the seam allowances go in opposite directions than to have seam allowances go toward the darker fabric.

Press the petal seams toward the wedge.

Gather the circle opening of this unit to fit the circle cut from figure 5. Use a long basting stitch and a ¼" seam. Arrange the gathers in the petals only, so that the narrow ends of the wedges are perfectly flat.

Mark the circle cut from figure 5 in 8 equal sections.

Match and pin the narrow ends of the wedges to the circle marks. Pin the center of each gathered petal to ensure security and the flatness of the circle. Repeat for all 15 Dahlia blocks.

Detail of Quilting

139

Join 4 triangular segments of figure 7 to a square made from figure 6, forming a 3″ square.

Next join 3 Dahlia blocks alternating with 4 strips of lattice to form a row. Repeat for 4 remaining rows. Complete the quilt top by joining the rows horizontally with alternating strips of lattice and small pieced squares.

For side panels, attach 1 red triangle to 1 white triangle (narrowest end of red to widest end of white), and continue until 15 pairs have been joined. Join 10 pairs for the bottom edge of quilt. Attach completed panels to sides and lower edge of quilt.

Last, use 2 white triangles slightly larger than the others to fill in the bottom corners.

All of the above construction can be machine-stitched.

Hand-quilting can be according to stitching lines and/or any additional design the quilter chooses.

The finished quilt measures 94″ × 108″.

Quilting directions and templates are given with permission of Susan Aylsworth Murwin and Suzzy Chalfant Payne, authors of *Quick and Easy Patchwork,* published by Dover Press.

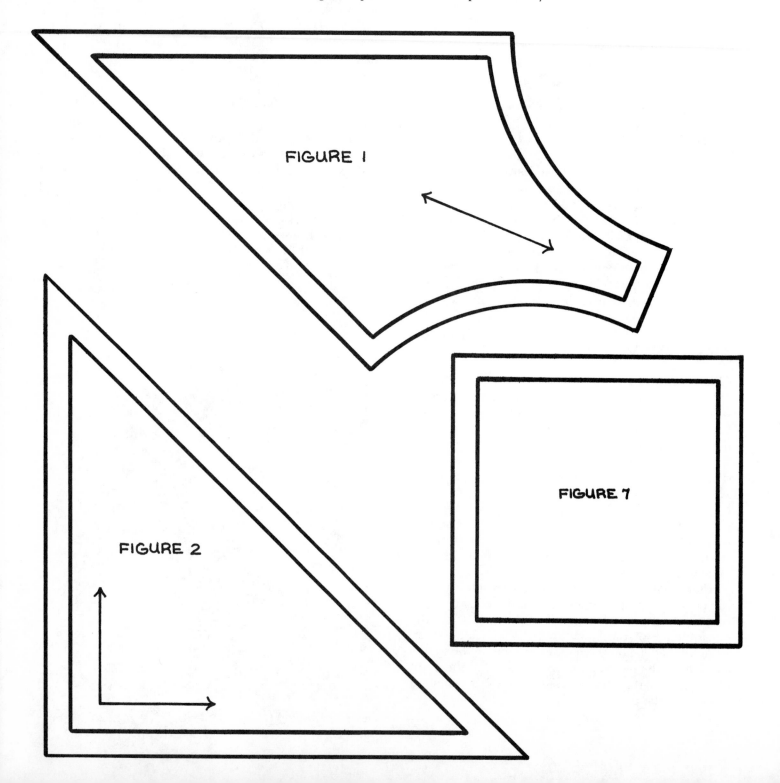

FIGURE 1

FIGURE 2

FIGURE 7

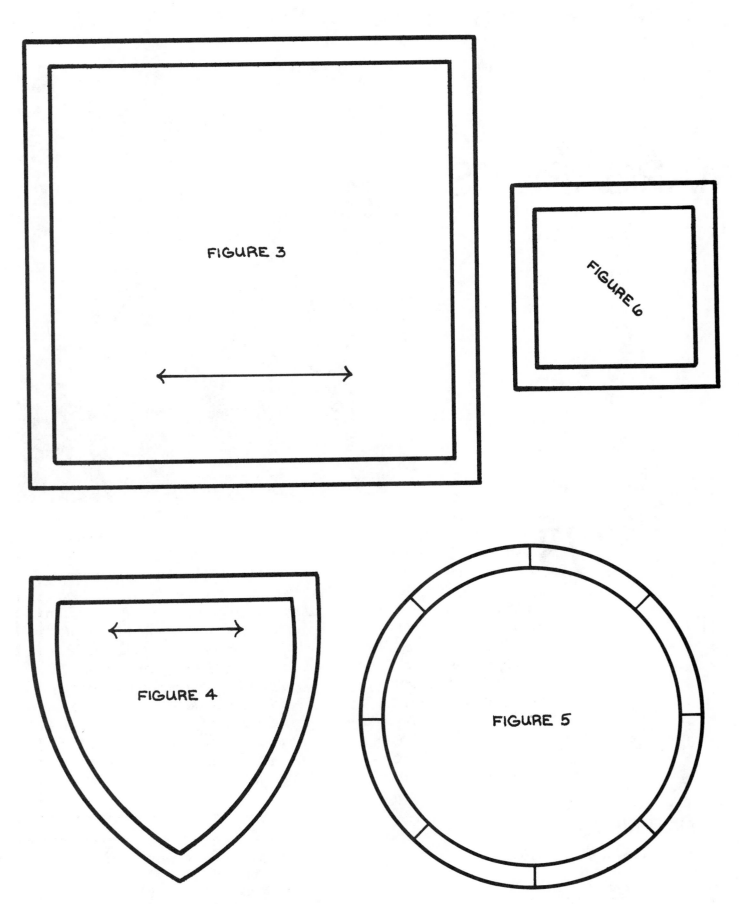

FIGURE 3

FIGURE 6

FIGURE 4

FIGURE 5

SUSAN BRAYMAN · *Jamestown, Rhode Island*

MARGARET'S STAR

"*B*est thing I ever did!" is how Susan Brayman described her decision to learn to quilt when a friend called her and said she had made arrangements for a teacher to come to her home to teach a group of women.

During the year that Susan worked on this prizewinning quilt, her mother would visit frequently and remark on how beautifully it was turning out. Susan told her that she planned to sell it, but her real plan was to give it to her mother. She completed it in time for Mother's Day, 1982, and really surprised her mother by presenting the gift in a garbage bag.

Margaret's Star *was originally* Martha's Star, *but Susan renamed it for her mother. It won First Prize for pieced quilts at the Rocky Hill State Fair and also Best of Show the same year. Susan has found learning to quilt with two metal thimbles and a hoop to be one of the most helpful techniques. "Sure saves on sore fingers. I used to have to stop when the pain was too much. Now I can quilt till my eyes close."*

MATERIALS

All fabrics used are 100 percent cotton:
  White—¾ yard
  Pink print—2⅝ yards

Light aqua print—3½ yards
Dark aqua print—1 yard
6 yards of a complementary fabric for backing

CUTTING GUIDE

Cut long borders first to be sure you have enough fabric. Templates do *not* include seam allowances.

Color A, white cotton, cut:
Figure 1–48

Color B, pink print, cut:
Figure 2–48
Figure 3–48
2 strips 5½″ × 90½″ for border (*includes seam allowance*)
2 strips 5½″ × 72½″ for border (*includes seam allowance*)

Color C, light aqua print, cut:
Figure 1–48
Figure 2–48
Figure 3–48
17 strips 3½″ × 15½″ for latticework (*includes* seam allowance)
2 strips 3½″ × 80½″ for border (*includes seam allowance*)
2 strips 3½″ × 62½″ for border (*includes seam allowance*)

Color D, dark aqua print, cut:
Figure 2–96
Figure 4–6
2 strips 5½″ × 100½″ for border (*includes seam allowance*)
2 strips 5½″ × 82½″ for border (*includes seam allowance*)

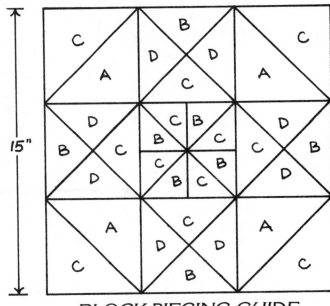

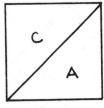
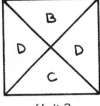
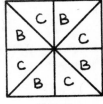

BLOCK PIECING GUIDE

Unit 1   Unit 2   Unit 3

ASSEMBLY

This quilt was machine-pieced and hand-quilted. The quilt consists of twelve 15″ blocks. The lattice is pieced with 3″ squares. Three outside borders are added. Quilt is bound with either purchased binding or self-binding.

Each 15″ block consists of:
4 Unit 1 squares
4 Unit 2 squares
1 Unit 3 square

Following the Block Piecing Guide, sew these 5″ squares together to form the 15″ block.

With a 3″ × 15″ lattice strip between blocks, sew the 15″ blocks into 4 rows of 3 units each.

Sew three rows, each consisting of 3 strips 3″ × 15″ joined with two 3″ squares between strips.

Join quilt together, alternating row of blocks with row of strips.

Sew inner border (color C) to quilt, matching centers. You will have uneven ends at borders. Enough extra has been allowed so that you can miter all three borders at one time.

Cut backing in half horizontally and sew together along long sides. Baste backing, batting, and top together.

Quilting. Quilt star shape in outline quilting ¼" away from seam allowance. White triangles are quilted with lines 1" apart. The 3" square in the latticework is quilted with a diamond inside and 2 larger diamonds outside. A quilted diamond joins these areas.

The finished quilt measures 82" × 100".

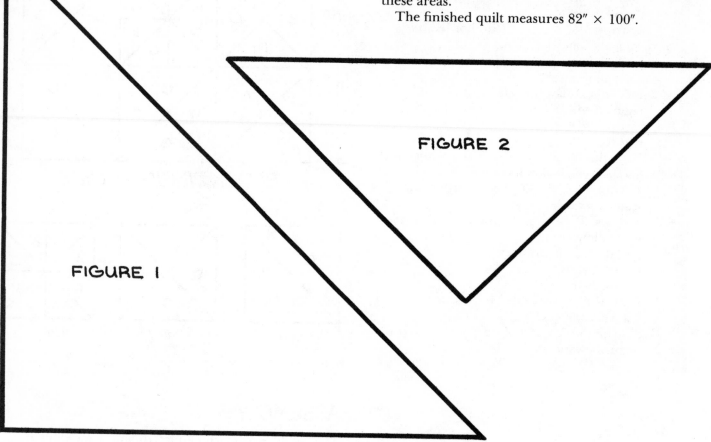

FIGURE 1

FIGURE 2

Template Figures do not include seam allowance

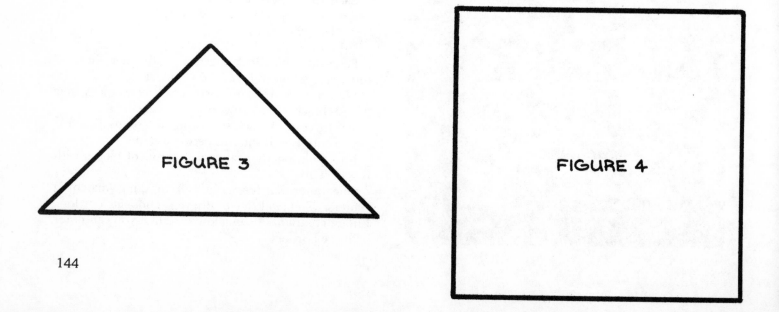

FIGURE 3

FIGURE 4

SOUTHERN ROSE

*T*he blue floral print and blue pinstripe borders that surround the central medallion and are repeated around the outer appliqué, and the outer two borders—one solid and one in a contrasting design—are some of the rich details that have been successfully combined in this quilt.

Southern Rose, a Rose of Sharon variation named by the quiltmaker, has won numerous prizes including First Place in appliqué at the South Carolina State Fair and two awards at the Smoky Mountain Quilt competition, including the People's Choice award.

When Nan Tournier's mother purchased twelve star blocks at a garage sale for fifty cents and gave them to her daughter, little did she realize what a remarkable investment she had made. Nan, who is the first in her family to quilt, went on to learn quilting from the one book available in the local library, and eventually taught her mother to quilt.

Nan chose this pattern from a 1934 quilt contest booklet. She has been quilting since 1969 and entering competitions since 1978.

"Don't be afraid to make mistakes—fabric is very forgiving," she urges, "and always prewash and machine-dry your fabrics before cutting them."

MATERIALS

All fabrics are 100 percent cotton. Approximately 1 yard of fabric is needed of each of the following colors: medium blue, dusty rose, and butter yellow. You will need 3 yards of avocado green, and 12 yards of unbleached muslin for the top and backing of the quilt. In addition to these solid colors, 2 prints are used: 2 yards of a blue pinstripe, and 1 yard of a soft blue-and-yellow floral print. The green solid is also used for a narrow bias binding in the quilt. Dacron batting.

CUTTING GUIDE

Just as in a medallion quilt, *Southern Rose* is cut and measured in stages as it is sewn, beginning with the appliqué blocks in the center. Length and width can be adjusted to fit your bed as the piece grows from border to border.

Add ¼″ seam allowance to all pieces and measurements given.

From unbleached muslin, cut:
  4 blocks 24″ square
  4 right triangles 30″ × 30″ × 42″
  2 strips 7″ × 73″
  2 strips 7″ × 101″
  1 strip 12″ × 66″
  2 strips 5″ × 106″
  1 strip 5″ × 90″

From blue-and-yellow floral print, cut:
  4 strips 2″ × 54″
  4 strips 2″ × 66″

From blue pinstripe, cut:
  8 strips ½″ × 54″
  8 strips ½″ × 66″

For each block, cut:
  Figure A–1 in blue
  Figure B–1 in yellow
  Figure C–1 in pink
  Figure D–1 in blue-and-yellow floral print
  Figure E–4 in green
  Figure F–8 in green
  Figure G–8 in pink
  Figure H–4 in blue pinstripe
  Figure I–4 in blue
  Figure J–4 in blue-and-yellow floral print
  Figure K–16 in green
  8 side stems, cut freehand to fit space

There are 4 complete blocks plus 4 half-blocks.
  For center of medallion cut 1 small rose and 4 leaves to cover seam:
  Figure I–1 in blue
  Figure J–1 in blue-and-yellow floral print
  Figure K–4 in green

FULL QUILT PIECING GUIDE

ASSEMBLY

The center medallion consists of 4 large rose blocks (the Appliqué Placement Guide shows 1 block) sewn together with a small rose and 4 leaves appliquéd in the center where the 4 seams meet. This 48″ square is bordered with a 3″ blue-and-yellow floral strip sandwiched between two ½″ blue pinstripe strips.

Four large muslin right triangles (30″ × 30″ × 42″) with simplified half-block floral appliqués are bordered with the same 3 borders, then sewn off-center to the central medallion. To help lengthen the quilt, the medallion meets these sections at top and bottom, but overlaps them at the sides, extending into the 7″ plain muslin border which is sewn on next.

Finally, a 5″ wide pieced border is added using the print fabrics, the green fabric, and the muslin. The diagram below shows the final border design. The sides consist of pieces cut from figures 1 and 2, then 1-reversed and Figure 2 sewn upside down to the first set. Continue sewing these pairs to get the length of border needed. The bottom 2 corner blocks are sewn to the 16 pairs of border units to create the bottom border. The top of the quilt does not have a pieced border, since this area is over and behind the pillow. A plain muslin border is sewn here.

The quilting outlines each appliqué shape, and the white muslin borders are quilted with feathery scrolls (see page 82). 1″-grid quilting is used on all background areas.

The finished quilt is approximately 90″ × 106″.

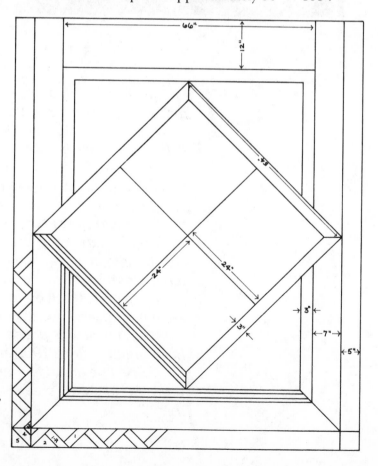

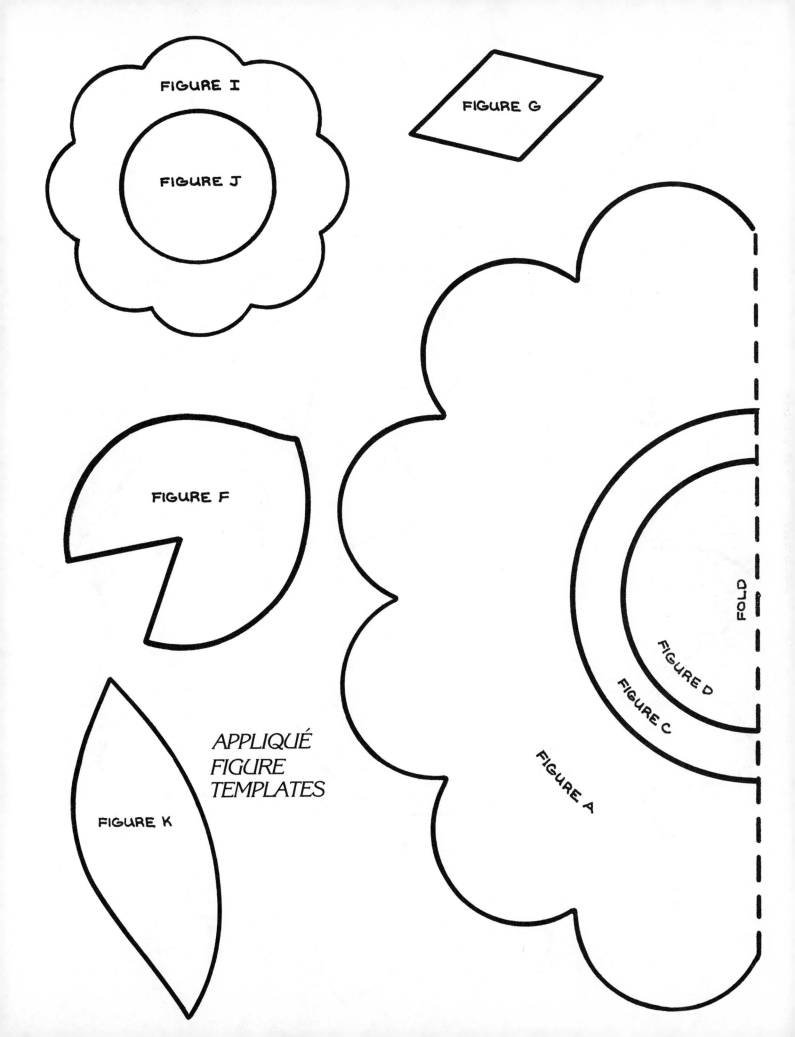

FIGURE I

FIGURE J

FIGURE G

FIGURE F

FIGURE D

FIGURE C

FOLD

FIGURE A

APPLIQUÉ
FIGURE
TEMPLATES

FIGURE K

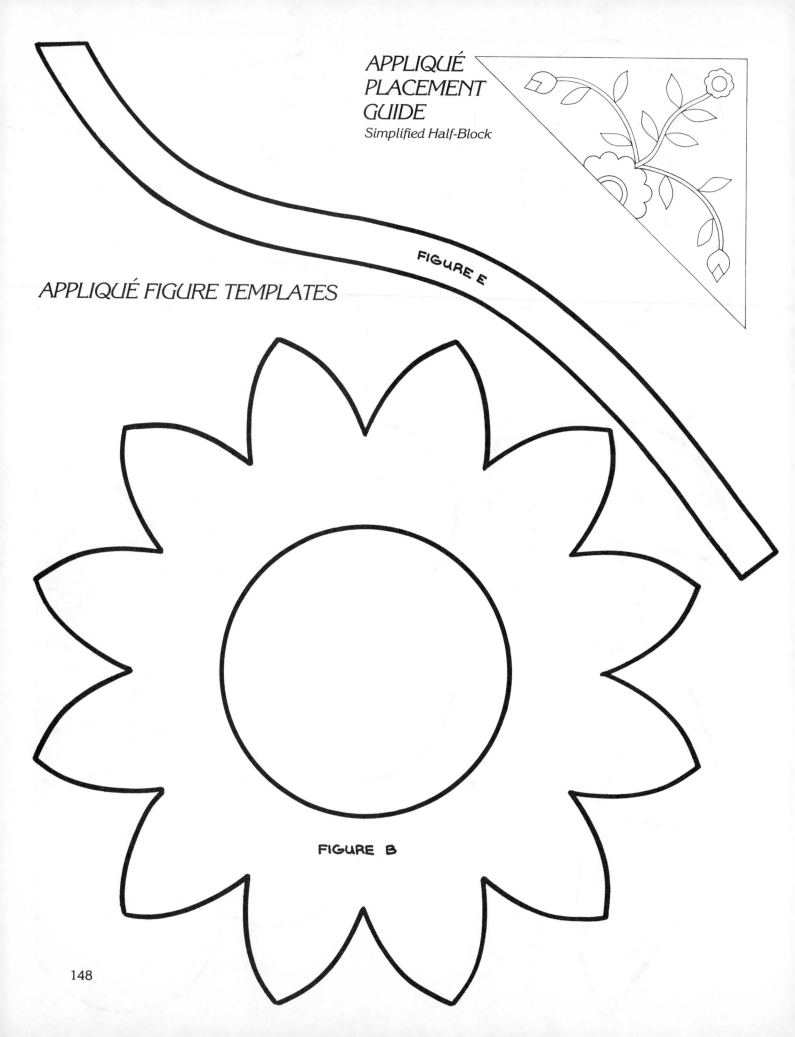

APPLIQUÉ
PLACEMENT
GUIDE
Simplified Half-Block

FIGURE E

APPLIQUÉ FIGURE TEMPLATES

FIGURE B

TEMPLATES FOR PIECING BORDER (Add seam allowance)

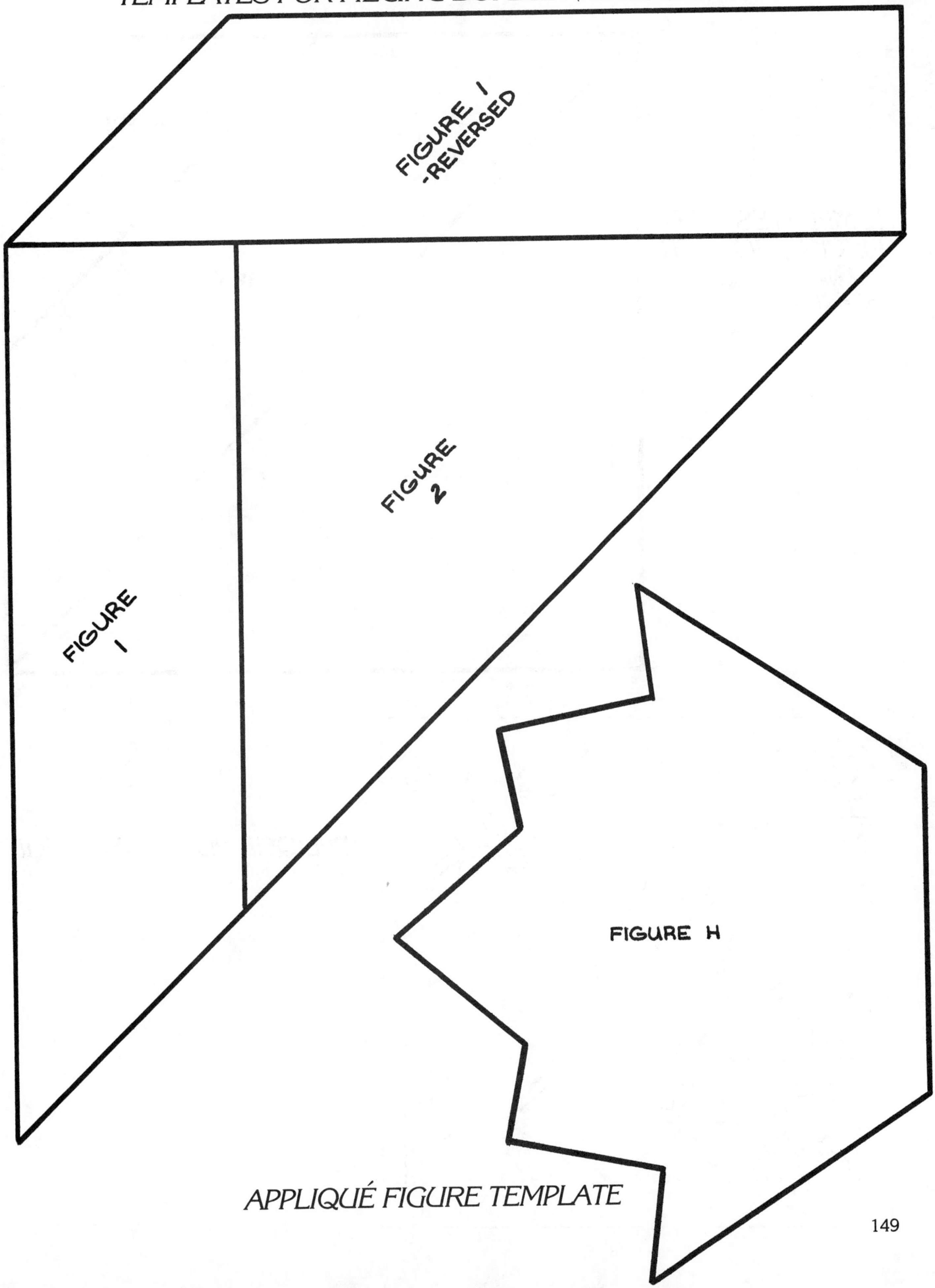

FIGURE 1
-REVERSED

FIGURE 2

FIGURE 1

FIGURE H

APPLIQUÉ FIGURE TEMPLATE

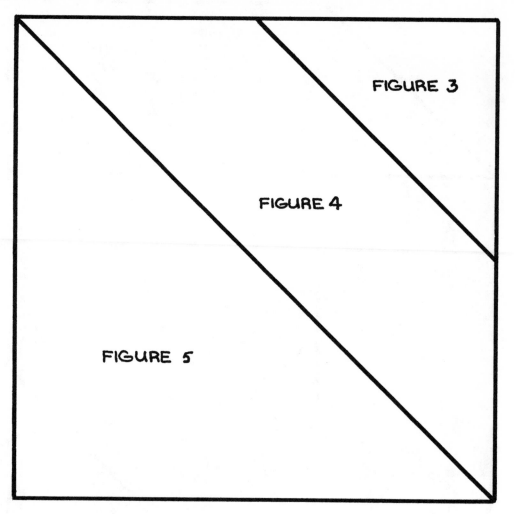

TEMPLATES FOR PIECING BORDER

(Add seam allowance)
corner block.

FIGURE 3

FIGURE 4

FIGURE 5

APPLIQUÉ PLACEMENT GUIDE
One Block

ARLENE TOWLER · *Miller, South Dakota*

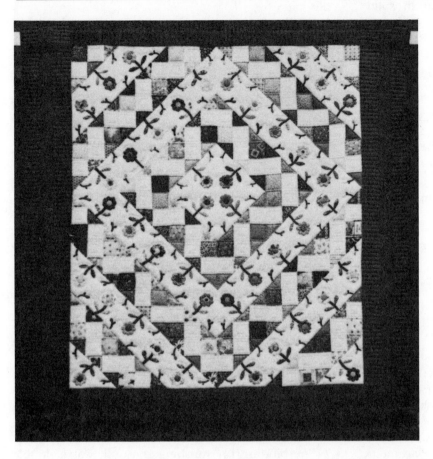

SUMMER FRAGRANCE

*A*fter twenty-three years of "do-it-yourself" quilting, Arlene Towler had an opportunity to take some lessons. She drove seventy miles each way to attend class, and "had a delightful time." For the last two years she has been teaching quilt-top classes.

Quilting is not a family tradition in Arlene's family. "I am the only one in my generation to quilt," she says.

Her Summer Fragrance has won First Prize in the appliqué and pieced category at the Columbia Mall Quilting Contest. Arlene has collected many First Prizes for several of her quilts at the Hand County Fair and the South Dakota State Fair.

While Arlene was piecing Summer Fragrance, her father became seriously ill. "I took my quilting along and as I sat in the intensive-care waiting room with my mother, I finished piecing the top. A couple of days later a lady who had also been in the waiting room came up to me and told me what therapy it was for her to see me working on the quilt top with its bright colors and we talked about quilting."

Arlene had seen a pattern for this quilt and chose it both because it was a good way to use up scraps and because it combines piecing and appliqué.

She has made twenty-three quilts and given thirteen away. Her advice to beginning quilters is, "Just get started and enjoy it."

MATERIALS

Cottons and cotton blends in white and in solid colors. At least 3 different printed fabrics. This is a good quilt for using up scraps. Use an extra thick batt to add dimension to flowers in quilt.

The quilt consists of 42 blocks. Templates and measurements do *not* include seam allowances.

For each block, cut:
- 1 white right triangle—half of a 12" square
- Figure 1—three 4" squares: 1 in print or color, 2 in white
- Figure 2—3 triangles: 1 in one print, 2 in another print
- Figure 3—1 flower in same print or color as figure 1
- Figure 4—1 flower center
- Figure 5—2 large leaves in same print as pair of triangles cut from figure 2
- Figure 6—4: 2 buds in same print as single triangle cut from figure 2, and 2 leaves

Cut various scraps of print fabrics for stems.

ASSEMBLY

On 1 of the large white triangles, appliqué the stems, leaves, buds, and large flowers according to Placement Diagram. The stems are made from bias strips using the continuous bias-binding method.

Next, appliqué the second 12" triangle with the 3 squares and 3 triangles as shown in the Placement Diagram.

The 2 white triangles are then joined together to make a 12" square block. Following the above instructions, appliqué and join 84 triangles to make the 42 blocks.

Set the 4 center blocks together and work out the most pleasing pattern for the remainder of the blocks, or follow the Piecing Diagram. (In Mrs. Towler's quilt, she placed the pieced part of the block as a walkway through the rows of flowers.)

A 10" × 72" navy border is added at top and bottom of quilt. A 10" × 84" border is added at both sides to complete top.

Because of the thick batt used in this quilt, it is important to baste the 3 layers together, especially if using a hoop. Mrs. Towler started the basting in the center of the quilt and worked out to the edge, basting lines from 12 to 18 inches apart both on the horizontal and vertical. Then quilting may begin.

Quilt 3 rows around the large flower, 1 row at the edge of the flower and the other 2 rows ¼" apart. The edge of the center of the flower is quilted.

Quilt 2 rows around the bud and stem, one row at the edge and the second ¼" away.

The large white triangle is quilted along the long bias seam where the two 12" triangles are stitched together.

Within the 3 small print triangles and the 1 print square, quilting is ¼" from the seam. Quilting is also done on the 2 white squares ¼" from the seam, and a 2" square is quilted in the center of each.

For the border, a rope effect was used.

The binding for finishing the quilt was a double thickness of the continuous bias binding.

The finished quilt measures 92" × 104".

PIECING GUIDE (one block)

152

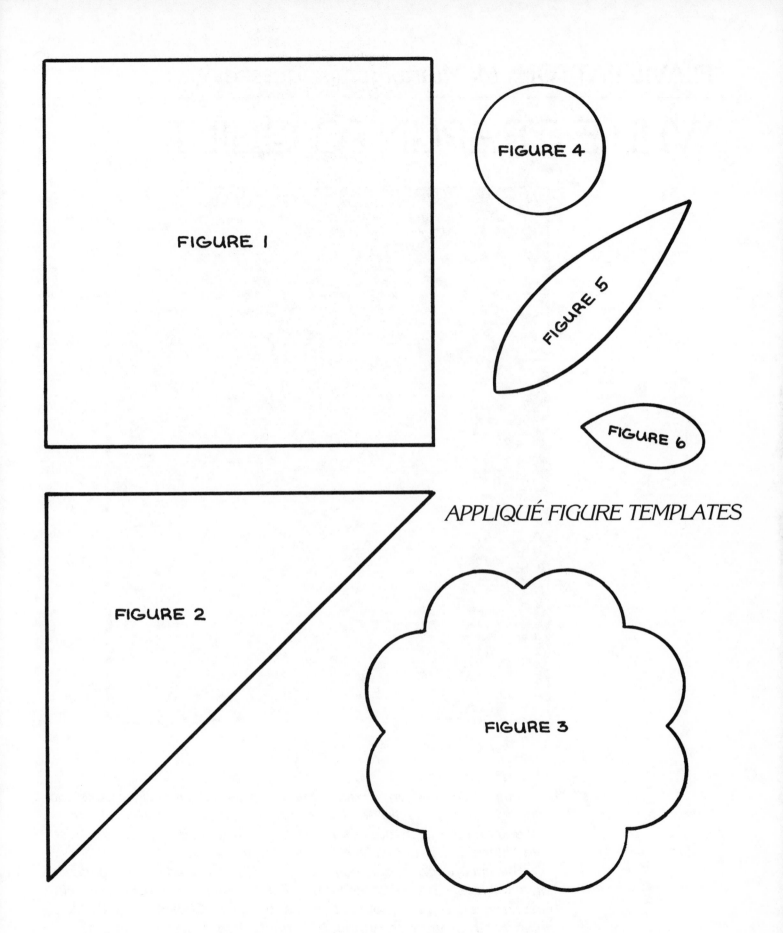

FIGURE 1

FIGURE 2

FIGURE 3

FIGURE 4

FIGURE 5

FIGURE 6

APPLIQUÉ FIGURE TEMPLATES

153

FLAVIL PATTON · *McMinnville, Tennessee*

WHITE TRAPUNTO QUILT

*F*lavil Patton really began his quilting career after he retired eight years ago. Although he saw it firsthand at home on the farm where both his mother and grandmother were quilters, he began quilting only after taking classes with Mildred Locke in Bell Buckle, Tennessee.

She encouraged him to complete a quilt that he had made a pattern for, and it was exhibited at the World's Fair in Knoxville. It went on to win First Prize in the whole-cloth category and Judges' Choice over all quilts entered at the Thirteenth Annual National Quilt Show.

Flavil likes working in cotton but now is trying some pure silk for a *new quilting venture. He advises beginners to find "the best teacher in a radius of one hundred miles and attend all classes. Do your best work. Press to get quality, not quantity."*

He does his quilting in Florida during the winter and back home in Tennessee during the rest of the year. He has been entering competitions only for the last three years, but has come away with top prizes in every contest he has entered.

Flavil gives emphasis to his quilting by using a raised trapunto effect, which is highly visible in the photograph below where the quilt was held up to the sunlight.

Although some recent interest has been shown in working in trapunto, most current pieces are usually contemporary designs. Mr. Patton's exacting white-on-white prizewinner is a unique example of using a traditional pattern with trapunto quilting.

BLUE JEAN QUILT

A genuine piece of folk art, Blue Jean Quilt *is also a family project that utilizes not only worn blue jeans fabric from the children's clothing, but the ideas and encouragement of the entire family. It holds a wealth of family history and reflects interests shared by all the members of this household.*

Blue Jean Quilt, Mrs. Russ Cox's first quilt, won First Prize and Best of Show at the Kerr County and the Gillespie County Fair, as well as First Prize and Best of Show at the Texas State Fair and the Mountain Mist Outstanding Quilt award.*

Though she learned stitching as a child, Pearl did not make a quilt until she decided to do something with all the cut-off jeans that she had saved from her three sons over many years. Pearl had never seen a denim quilt when she began her project, although she has since seen others. Blue Jean Quilt *is made entirely by hand, and has nine to twelve stitches per inch in the actual quilting. Because of the combination of the thickness of the jeans fabric, batting, and quilt backing, Pearl was not able to do any running stitches. She had to put the needle through all the thicknesses and "poke it back up for each stitch." For the last ten days before the county fair, she frequently worked eight to ten hours a day to finish it in time for the competition.*

"The quilt just grew like Mopsie," says Pearl. "Each 'big' square has nine 'little' ones and each one is different. Some are old toys; favorite birds and flowers; animals; butterflies; the family's zodiac signs and birthdates; and even favorite nursery rhymes.

"I have always loved stitchery of any kind, and learned by trying." For aspiring quilters, Pearl has this suggestion, "Do it if you enjoy it. There is a great satisfaction in creating something." The quilt took a total of 1,752 hours to complete.

MATERIALS

A box of cut-off legs from faded blue jeans. Fabric was faded to a variety of lovely shades of blue.

CUTTING GUIDE

Because fine embroidery like Pearl Cox's is more easily accomplished on large pieces of fabric (which are more readily held in an embroidery hoop) it is best to mark fabric, embroider as desired, and then cut into patches. The finished quilt is composed of twenty 18″ squares, each made up of nine 6″ squares. These 18″ blocks are separated by a narrow border of 3″ × 6″ rectangles joined by 3″ squares. Measurements and templates do *not* include seam allowances.

> Figure 1–180
> Figure 2–147
> Figure 3–30

ASSEMBLY

This quilt is entirely hand-pieced, hand-appliquéd and hand-embroidered. All designs are hand-drawn, then translated into bright, colorful needlework pictures. Each of the 20 large blocks has a theme which is illustrated with nine individual drawings. For example, one is a Christmas square that includes the boys' old rocking horse, Mr. Cox's childhood spinning top, Pearl's old teddy bear, and a bear on wheels from Pearl's grandparents' childhood days.

Once the 9 squares for each of the 20 blocks have been completed and assembled, they are joined with narrow denim strips, embroidered with random, decorative designs, to form the complete quilt top.

Batting, a neutral backing, and bias binding in navy blue complete the quilt, which is then embroidered with a contrasting thread along the joining lines.

Template Figures do not include seam allowance

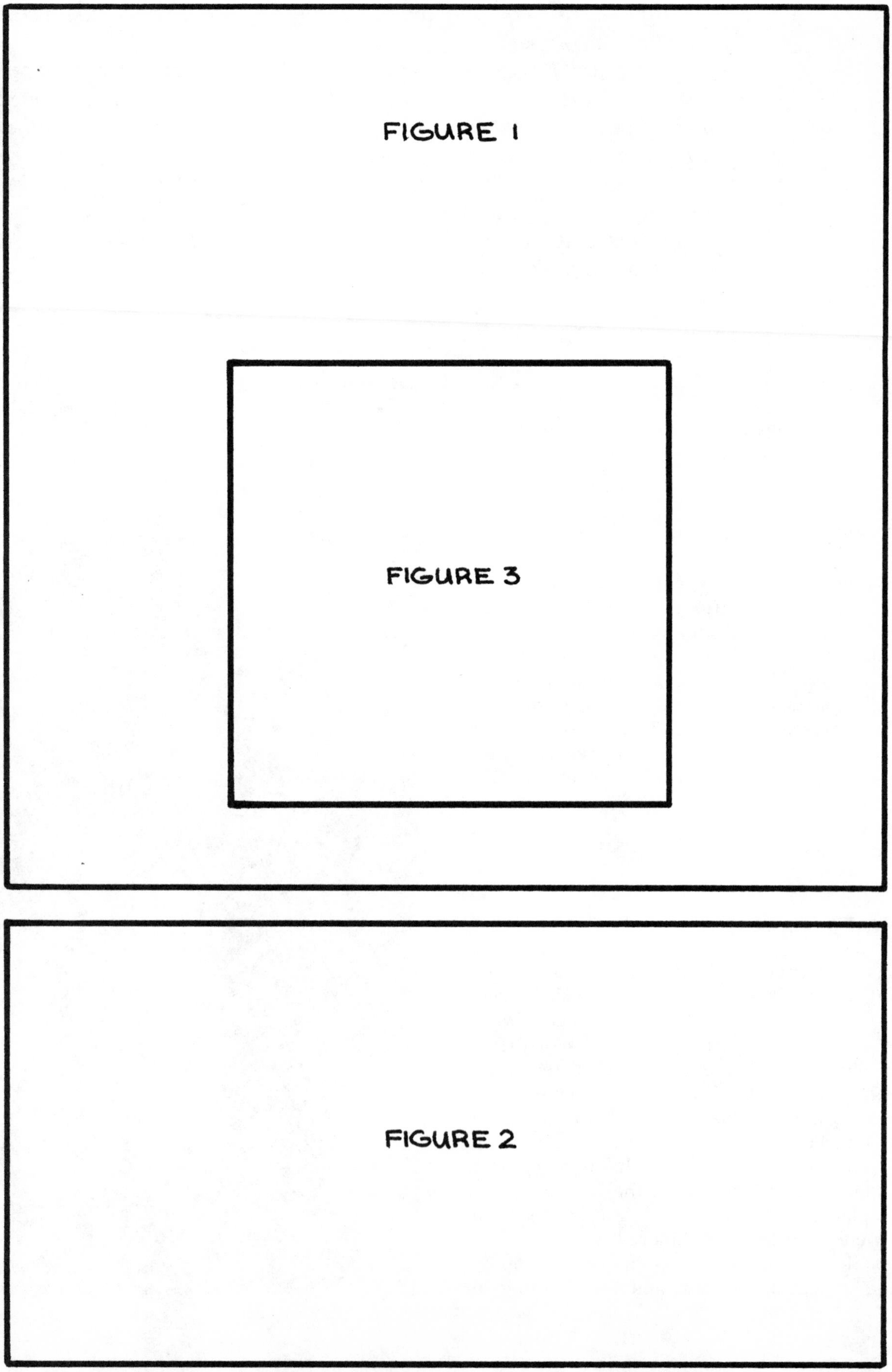

FIGURE 1

FIGURE 3

FIGURE 2

HELEN N. ESKELSON · *Salt Lake City, Utah*

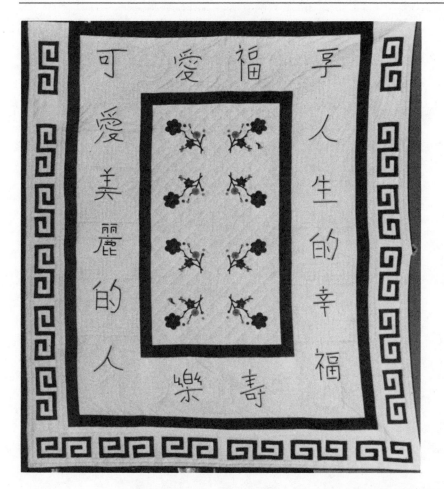

可愛 愛 福 亨
可 人
愛 生
美 的
麗 幸
的 福
人
樂 壽

ORIENTAL BLOSSOM

*H*elen Eskelson's Oriental Blossom *quilt won First Prize and the sweepstakes at the Salt Lake County Fair, as well as First Prize at the Utah State Fair.*

"I learned to quilt at home from my Aunt Lillian. When Saturdays came around, I quilted for my mother to get out of helping with the housework.

"As of June 1983, I have quilted 1,350 quilts in all sizes. After forty-one years, my husband still complains about helping me to turn the quilt."

Helen has made many other prizewinning quilts and even two quilts of all the ribbons she has collected over the years. She is especially proud that one of her quilts was purchased by Marie Osmond last year.

Her suggestion to the novice quilter is, "Start with a small quilt like a baby quilt that is easy to do. I started with a double size and it took a year to finish!"

One of the unique aspects of this all-cotton broadcloth quilt is the Chinese calligraphy, created with two shades of bias tape for a three-dimensional look. Clockwise from the top, they say: Love, Prosperity, Enjoy One's Life, Happiness and Long Life, and A Beautiful and Lovely Individual. Expert embroidery in the central floral motif and subtle quilting designs that suggest Chinese pictographs complete the marriage between Eastern delicacy and Western folk art tradition.

JOAN DYER · *Belvidere, Vermont*

COMPASS AND DOGWOOD

*I*t comes as no surprise after viewing **Compass and Dogwood** *to learn that Joan Dyer has a Ph.D. in mathematics. Her adaptation of two quilt patterns—Mariner's Compass and Dogwood—is based on square patches of one inch.*

This prizewinner has collected top awards from Vermont to California including First Prize in the hand-piecing category at the International Quilt Exhibit at Rancho Santa Fe, California, and First Prize in the category of medallion/hand-made by a non-professional at the 1983 National Quilt Association Show in Bell Buckle, Tennessee.

Joan likes to have some kind of sewing project in progress at all times. She took up the challenge of quiltmaking when her stepdaughter asked for a quilt as a high school graduation gift thirteen years ago. Since then she has honed her skills and each new quilt brings with it new challenges.

"I don't allow myself to start more than one project in an area at a time. If there is a quilt in progress I can start a needlework project or another idea, but not another quilt. That way I'll be sure to finish it."

Joan taught at the university level for many years, but recently decided to take a leave and has accepted a position in industry. In both of her "careers," math and quilting, she is always seeking new challenges.

Salishan Tree by Roberta Cook, page 166. (PHOTO BY EDWIN G. COOK)

details of *Blue Jean Quilt* by
Pearl Cox, page 156. (PHOTO
BY B. MICHAEL COX)

Jacob's Fan by Elizabeth W. Daugherty, page 172. (PHOTO BY WEST VIRGINIA DEPARTMENT OF CULTURE AND HISTORY)

Compass and Dogwood by Joan Dyer, page 160. (PHOTO BY JOAN DYER)

OPPOSITE
Tulips and Trumpets by Anne
J. Oliver, page 164. (PHOTO BY
DOROTHY CHATFIELD BUFFMIRE,
PHOTOGRAPHED AT THE
WOODLAWN PLANTATION)

Summer Fragrance by Arlene Towler, page 151. (PHOTO BY JOAN'S STUDIO, MILLER, SOUTH DAKOTA)

MATERIALS

100 percent cotton fabrics in white, ivory, gold, aqua, and navy.

A tiny blue-and-gold print for 1″ borders and center of medallion.

CUTTING GUIDE

Templates do *not* include seam allowances.

For medallion, cut:

    Figure 1–8 in print fabric
    Figure 2–8 in navy
    Figure 3–8 in white
    Figure 4–8 in navy
    Figure 5–8 in navy
    Figure 6–16 in aqua
    Figure 7–32 in gold
    Figure 8–32 in navy
    Figure 9–32 in white
    Figure 10–32 in navy
    Figure 11–32 in white

For dogwood background—132 blocks 4″ square: 68 with white-on-navy star, 64 with navy-on-white star—cut:

    Figure A–528 in white and 528 in aqua
    Figure B–36 in white, 128 in navy
    Figure B *reversed*–136 in white, 128 in navy
    Figure C–256 in white, 272 in navy
    Figure D–136 in white, 128 in navy
    Figure E–264 in white
    Figure F–128 in white, 136 in navy

For border, cut:

    Figure 12–76 in navy
    Figure 13–72 in aqua
    Figure 14–36 in ivory
    Figure 15–72 in navy, 68 in ivory

For 1″ border around medallion and 1″ border around dogwood pattern, cut:

    Two 1″ strips of print fabric in each of the following lengths: 30″, 32″, 58″, 60″ (*not* including seam allowances)

ASSEMBLY

This quilt is assembled from the center out.

For medallion: Join all segments of figure 1 to form a small circle. Next stitch all segments of figures 2 and 3 into a ring and, pinning carefully to ensure proper alignment of points, set this ring around the circle of print fabric. Continuing in this fashion, piece and stitch the compass-point band and the two additional rings of navy and white, carefully setting the central circle into each new ring.

To complete medallion, describe a 30″ circle on a piece of gold fabric that will just contain it (30½″ × 30½″, *including* seam allowance) and mark a square framing the circle. Allowing ¼″ for seams, cut inside the marking to make a square frame. The compass medallion is then set inside this frame, yielding a 30″ square panel. Add the 1″ border in print fabric to yield a 32″ square.

Next piece all the dogwood squares for the background, according to Piecing Guide; 68 of the blocks

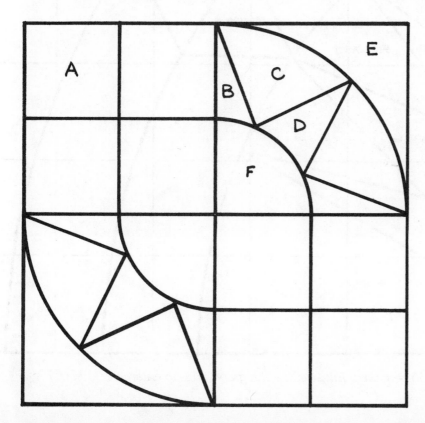

DOGWOOD TEMPLATE FIGURES AND PIECING GUIDE

(Add seam allowance)

will have white points set into a navy arc, 64 will have navy points set in a white background.

The background should be assembled in 8 pieces —4 rectangles that will abut the sides of the medallion, and 4 corner blocks. These guides show placement of the blocks, with "w" representing blocks with white points on a navy background and "n" representing blocks with navy points on a white background:

```
n w n w w n w n          w n w
w n w n n w n w          n w n
n w n w w n w n          w n w
```

Be sure to check the photograph often for proper placement of the dogwood blossoms when piecing

MEDALLION TEMPLATE FIGURES AND PIECING GUIDE
(Add seam allowance)

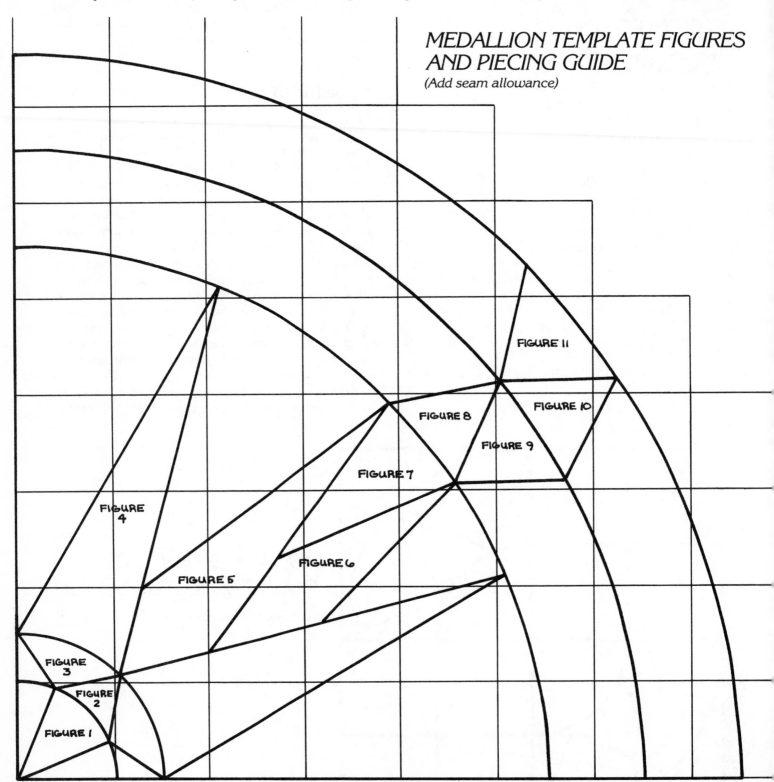

(shown at 50 percent of full size; use the graph lines to enlarge to full size)

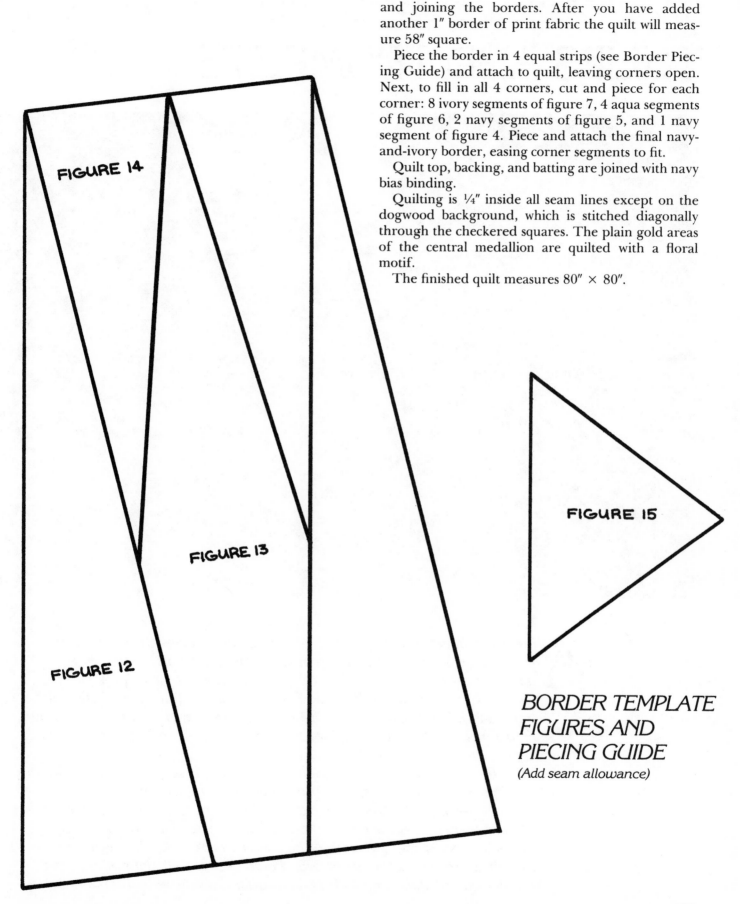

FIGURE 14

FIGURE 13

FIGURE 12

FIGURE 15

and joining the borders. After you have added another 1″ border of print fabric the quilt will measure 58″ square.

Piece the border in 4 equal strips (see Border Piecing Guide) and attach to quilt, leaving corners open. Next, to fill in all 4 corners, cut and piece for each corner: 8 ivory segments of figure 7, 4 aqua segments of figure 6, 2 navy segments of figure 5, and 1 navy segment of figure 4. Piece and attach the final navy-and-ivory border, easing corner segments to fit.

Quilt top, backing, and batting are joined with navy bias binding.

Quilting is ¼″ inside all seam lines except on the dogwood background, which is stitched diagonally through the checkered squares. The plain gold areas of the central medallion are quilted with a floral motif.

The finished quilt measures 80″ × 80″.

*BORDER TEMPLATE
FIGURES AND
PIECING GUIDE*
(Add seam allowance)

ANNE J. OLIVER · *Alexandria, Virginia*

TULIPS AND TRUMPETS

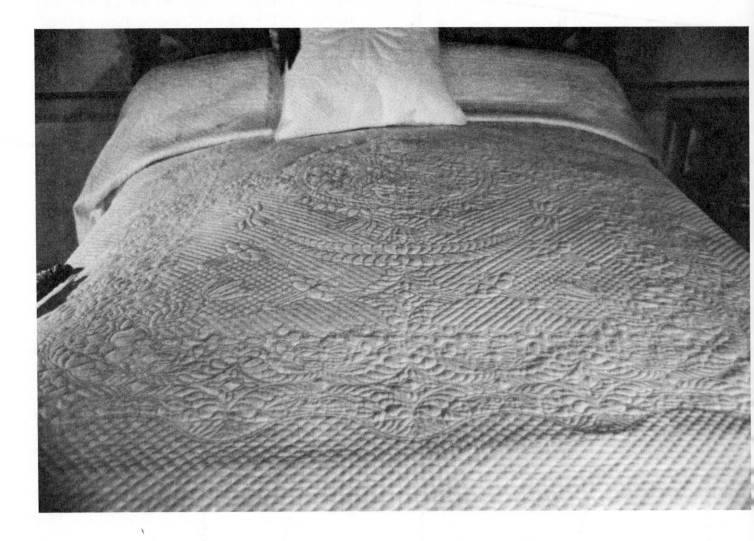

A magnificent version of the white-on-white quilt is Anne J. Oliver's Tulips and Trumpets. *Among the many awards this spectacular work has garnered are First Prize and Most Popular of Show at the Annual Needlework Exhibit, Woodlawn Plantation, Mt. Vernon, Virginia; First Prize in the International Quilt Show, San Diego; First Prize and Most Popular of Show, Fredericksburg, Virginia; and First Prize and Most Popular of Show at Bell Grove, Virginia.*

This is an original design, named by the quiltmaker, of a combination of tulips, which she loves, and trumpet vines. Anne likes to use contemporary designs in early American settings. When she entered the quilt in the Woodlawn Show, Anne received a call from a newspaper reporter about the Blue Ribbon she had won. Anne asked where the quilt was in the exhibit, and the reporter responded, "I didn't see a quilt; your pillow was on the bed and it won First Place." The quilt looked so much at home on the bed in the early American setting that the reporter had missed the star of the show.

With over twelve hundred hours of work involved, there were many times when things did not go smoothly. "Twice during the redesigning of particular areas that should have looked great but didn't, I heard the Monday morning trash truck and would have gladly thrown the quilt into the trash, if I could have got it off the frame. My quilting friend, Smokey, helped me get over the discouragement, and I finished."

Anne tells her students, "Get a quilting buddy to help you over the hurdles, especially when undertaking a long project like a quilt. Pace yourself. Expect to spend some time on your project each day, even if it is fifteen minutes, because fifteen times thirty equals seven and a half hours in a month, which is better than no time at all. Otherwise, three years later you will still be saying, 'I'll get started tomorrow.' I tell my students that I am their quilting friend, that they should call me whenever they need help. I remember them by their projects."

The design for this white-on-white quilt was created by making designs on white freezer paper, ironing them onto old file folders, and using these for templates. The central medallion was pieced first, then sections were added until the whole quilt was filled with designs. Then the quilt was put into the frame and quilted all over.

The fringe of the quilt was crocheted in three strips and sewed on securely, but can be taken off if the fringe does not last as long as the quilt. Early American fringe on most white work does not have directions so Anne had to improvise and create her own.

During the work she used about ten packets of needles, plus twelve large spools of quilting thread and fifteen skeins of fringe yarn.

SALISHAN TREE

A few years ago when her husband's job took them several states away from their home, Roberta Cook decided to plan a quilt that would ease their homesickness and be a reminder of the area they love. The Cooks own a beach house on the Oregon coast near a large resort called Salishan, the name of a now extinct Indian tribe of the area. The lodge uses a windswept tree as a logo, which became the starting point of Roberta's quilt.

"The tree is appliqué, and the rest is pieced from my original designs, with inspiration from Chris Edmonds [First Prize Quilts Kansas winner]. I tried to give the quilt an Indian look by using sawtooth patterns and including blue and purple, along with the blacks and browns. It has 1790 pieces; it took 891 hours to complete; and the quilting is ten stitches to the inch.

"Above the tree on the left the quilting represents the winds, on the right is the rain, and left and under the tree the quilting represents water."

Salishan Tree *has won a Blue Ribbon in the medallion category at the Santa Rosa, California, Quilt Show, as well as having won awards in all of the major Western Washington Fairs. At the Puyallup Fair, which is the seventh largest fair in the country, it won a Blue Ribbon, a Best-of-Category Ribbon and the Grand Champion Ribbon. Roberta, a self-taught quilter, has these recommendations for new quilters: "Take good lessons. Don't give up. Go to lots of shows. And pick a good pattern, even if hard, for a first quilt. If I had not had a good-looking pattern and good colors, I would never have made another one."*

After working most of her adult life in a bank, Roberta decided that when she retired she wanted to find an interest which would be totally removed from the mathematical world she had worked in for so long. Quilting and sewing, she decided, would be a total change. Little did she imagine how much math she would be using in her new avocation!

MATERIALS

Cotton/poly-blend fabrics, including 5 yards beige, 2½ yards purple, 2½ yards turquoise blue, 1¾ yards solid brown, 10 yards brown print, and 6½ yards black. Also, 10 spools sewing thread, 7½ spools quilting thread in five colors, one large batt, plus piecing as necessary.

CUTTING GUIDE

Measurements and templates do *not* include seam allowance.

From beige fabric, cut:

One 32½″ square for center medallion

Figure A–	96	Figure H–	4
Figure E–	12	Figure I–	72
Figure F–	208	Figure L–	4

From purple fabric, cut:

Figure A–	96	Figure F–	164
Figure E–	4	Figure N–	68

From turquoise blue, cut:

Figure A–	96	Figure J–	64
Figure B–	4	Figure K–	4

From solid brown cut:

Figure A–	96	Figure C–	8

From brown print, cut:

Figure A–	96	Figure G–	48
Figure D–	4		

Backing

From black, cut:

Figure A–	96	Figure M–	4
Figure F–	416	Figure N–	84

20 black strips for borders (all black-strip borders are mitered), 4 each of the following measurements:

#1. 1¾″ × 36½″ (32½″ + 4″ for miter)
#2. 2½″ × 50″ (44½″ + 5½″ for miter)
#3. 3″ × 65″ (58½″ + 6½″ for miter)
#4. 3″ × 82½″ (76″ + 6½″ for miter)
Binding: 2″ × 110″ (104″ + 6″ for miter)

ASSEMBLY

The 32½″ square medallion center is attached to the #1 black border.

Next assemble the first pieced border per Piecing Guide (p. 170). Then attach black border #2, in same manner as black border #1, mitering corners.

The sawtooth border follows by sewing 4 strips consisting of 24 blue triangles from figure A and 24 purple triangles from figure A joined together. Add corner unit, as shown below, for each side.

The black border #3 is then attached in the same manner as the previous two black borders.

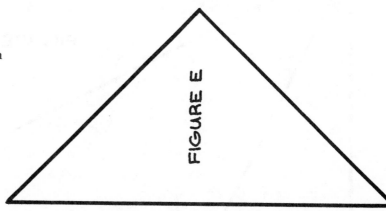

Template Figures do not include seam allowance
Sawtooth Border Corner Unit

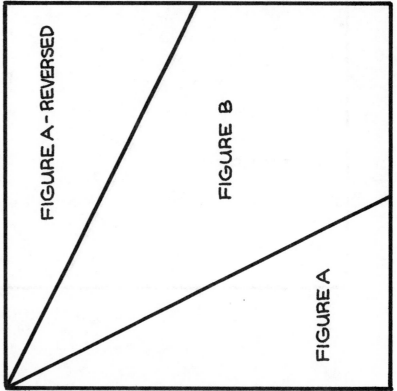

The third pieced border is composed of rectangles made by sewing solid brown, brown print, black and beige Figure A triangles together along their bias edges. Refer to photo in color section for placement. Finish corner w/four border units as shown below.

Attach black border #4.

For the final pieced border, refer to Piecing Guide. (Roberta started at right corner and worked left, feeling that it was easier for her.) There is no "beginning and ending" to this border, so pieces are sewn together as you go along in uneven units. It is slow and exacting. Points must match precisely. Check photo often.

To finish, add batting and backing and finish with a dark binding, with mitered corners.

Background of the tree was quilted to represent wind, rain and water. There is no pattern for the medallion, which was a hand-drawn design based

Third Pieced Border Corner Unit (Templates do not include seam allowance)

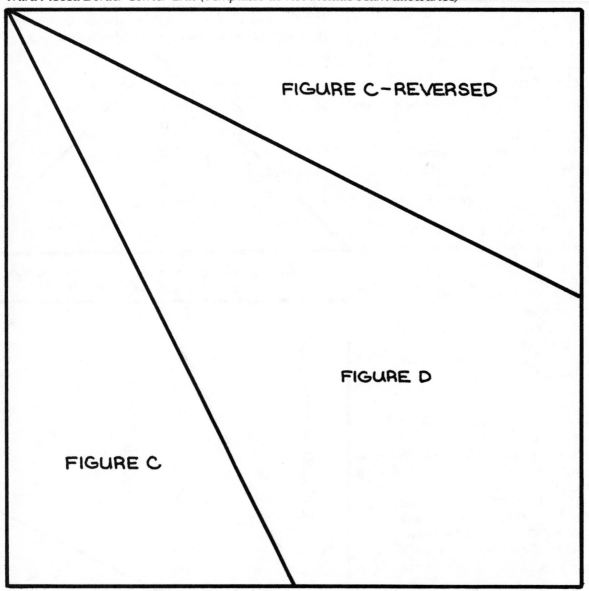

FIGURE C-REVERSED

FIGURE D

FIGURE C

on the resort logo, or the quilting. All other pieces were outline-quilted, with several additional lines measured accurately to assure the same distance between lines.

This difficult, detailed pattern requires precise measurements as no allowance is made for adjustment. All triangles have the long side on the straight grain of fabric.

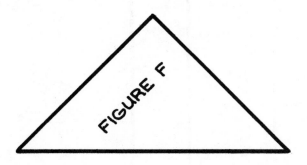

Template Figures do not include seam allowance

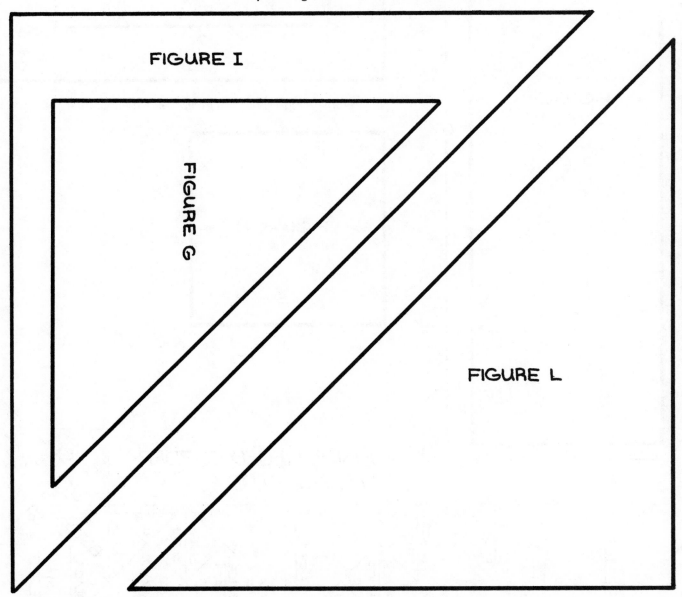

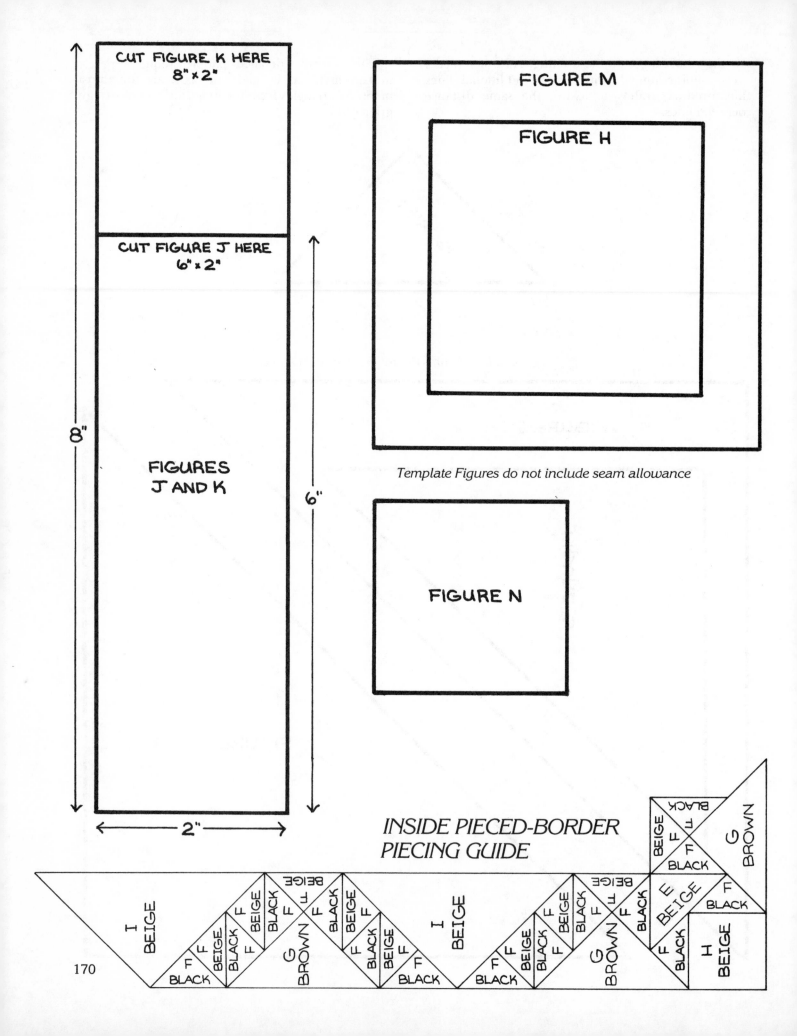

CUT FIGURE K HERE
8" x 2"

CUT FIGURE J HERE
6" x 2"

FIGURES
J AND K

8"

6"

2"

FIGURE M

FIGURE H

Template Figures do not include seam allowance

FIGURE N

*INSIDE PIECED-BORDER
PIECING GUIDE*

170

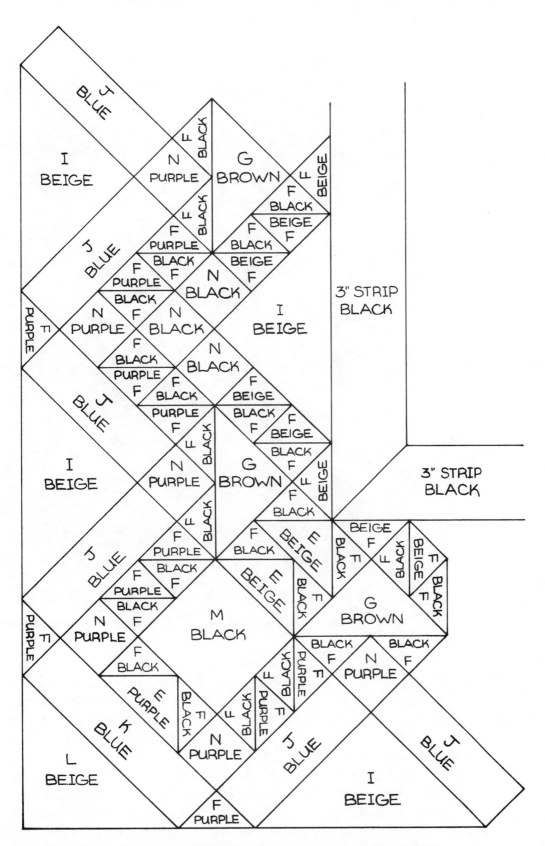

OUTSIDE PIECED-BORDER PIECING GUIDE

171

ELIZABETH W. DAUGHERTY · *Belmont, West Virginia*

JACOB'S FAN

*E*lizabeth's Daugherty's Jacob's Fan *won First Prize in traditional piecing at Quilts 1983, sponsored by the West Virginia Culture and History Center in Charleston. It has also won the People's Choice award at the Pleasants County Quilt Club Show, and First Prize and Best of Show at the Pleasants County Home Extension Quilt Show.*

Elizabeth has been quilting "off and on for forty to forty-five years," but began quilting more intensely in 1973 when her husband became ill and she began caring for him. She decided to make a quilt for each of her fourteen grandchildren, beginning with a grandson who was about to get married. After she finished the last of the fourteen quilts, Elizabeth went on to make a whole-cloth quilt, using unpieced yardage covered with the extensive quilting that symbolizes fine workmanship. This quilt also won First Prize and Best of Show locally.

In addition to making quilts for her family, Elizabeth works in a local quilt shop. Her suggestion to those who would like to learn to quilt is, "Find a good teacher and take classes, or get a good basic book and follow instructions."

MATERIALS

The colors specified follow Mrs. Daugherty's quilt; other color schemes may be used. 100 percent cotton fabrics:

 1⅜ yards solid blue for plain blocks
 4½ yards light blue for Fan blocks
 2 yards assorted blue prints for Fan blocks
 ¾ yard white for Jacob's Ladder blocks
 ¾ yard red for Jacob's Ladder blocks
 ⅔ yard each of two shades of blue for borders to
  be pieced of 2½" strips

CUTTING GUIDE

Measurements and templates *include* seam allowance. There are a total of 48 blocks, each 12" square, including:

 12 plain blocks
 28 Fan blocks
 8 Jacob's Ladder blocks

For each of the 12 plain blocks, cut a 12" square of solid blue fabric.

For each of the 28 Fan blocks, cut:

 Figure A–1 in light blue
 Figure B–6: 1 in red and 5 in various blue prints
  (8 different blues were used for cutting figure
  B)
 Figure C–1 in dark blue

For the Jacob's Ladder blocks, cut:

 Figure D–28: 14 in red, 14 in white
 Figure E–8: 4 in red, 4 in white
 2 strips 76" × 2" and 2 strips 100" × 2" in
  medium blue for first border
 2 strips 80" × 2" and 2 strips 104" × 2" in light
  blue print for outer border

ASSEMBLY

To assemble quilt, piece all blocks. Begin with the Fan blocks, which are pieced as follows: form the "fan" by joining 6 pieces of figure B: 5 random pieces of assorted prints and one red piece. Complete the block by fitting 1 piece of figure C into the smaller,

inside curve, and one piece of figure A along the outside curve. Complete all 28 fan blocks as above.

Next, piece Jacob's Ladder blocks. To piece, assemble 3 checkerboard squares, using 12 pieces of figure D: 6 in red and 6 in white. Arrange these 3 squares on a flat surface, with the corners of the *white* squares touching, forming a diagonal line. Using 4 red pieces of figure D and 4 red pieces of figure E to fill in the gaps, stitch together to form a solid diagonal strip. Piece 4 red and 4 white pieces of figure D into 2 checkerboard squares. Then, join 1 white piece of figure D to each of the 2 white squares in the 2 checkerboards. To each of the 2 checkerboard units, join 4 figure E triangles to form 2 large triangles, each with a red square at the top point. Stitch these to either side of the diagonal strip to complete the block.

When all pieced and plain blocks are complete, arrange them on table top or floor to assure proper positioning, according to pattern. Join all blocks, and add the 2 borders to finish. Miter corners.

To quilt, stitch ¼" inside seam lines on all pieced blocks. For large, curved light-blue print areas surrounding Fans, the quilting follows the curves at 1" intervals, creating concentric rings and arches. The plain blue blocks are quilted with a feathered design (see page 81) which is echoed in the first border. A braided chain finishes the outer border.

The finished quilt measures 80" × 104".

PIECING GUIDE

173

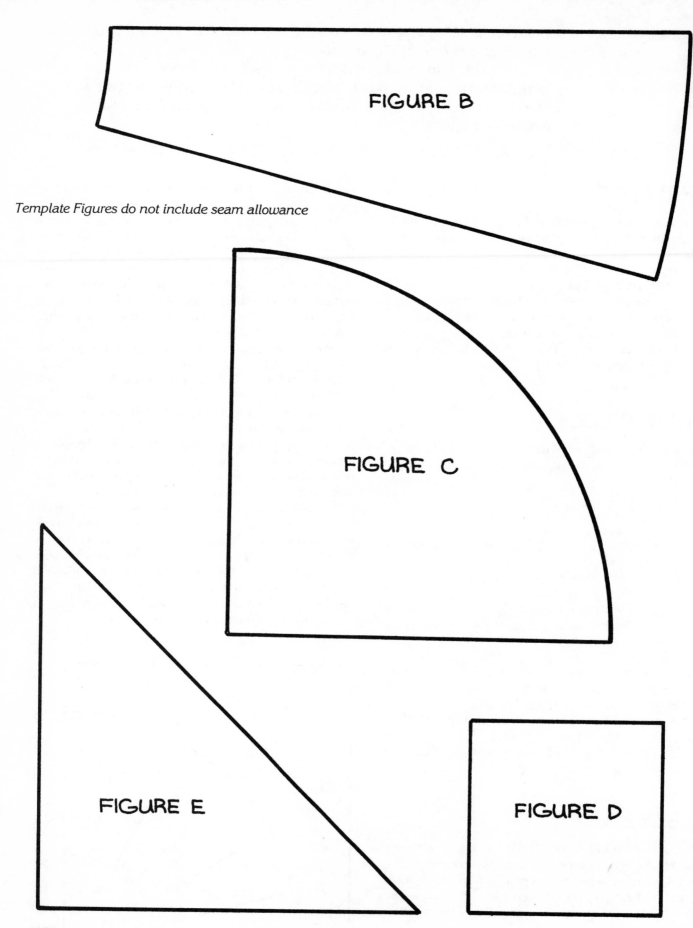

FIGURE B

Template Figures do not include seam allowance

FIGURE C

FIGURE E

FIGURE D

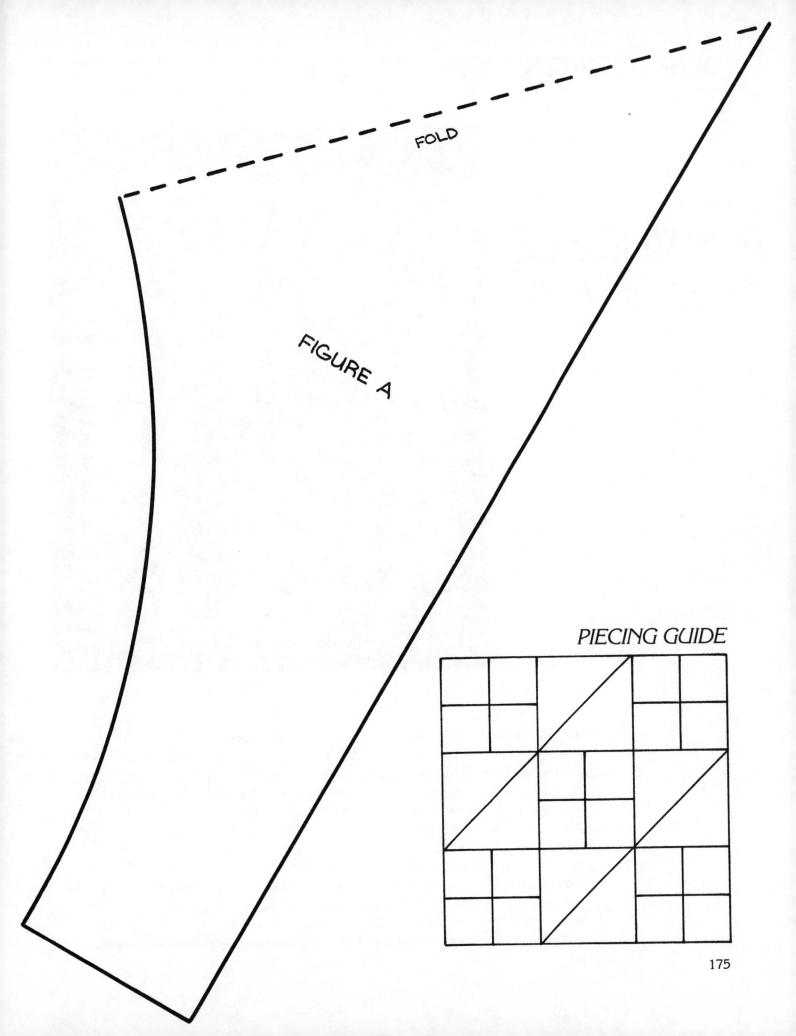

FOLD

FIGURE A

PIECING GUIDE

175

GENEVA WATTS · *Racine, Wisconsin*

PINWHEELS AND STARS

Geneva Watts has completed so many quilts and won such a large number of prizes with them that it was difficult just to choose one to include here. Pinwheels and Stars (with flying geese border) is a traditional quilt in many ways. For one thing, Geneva chose to make it because she wanted to use up scraps left from years of sewing for her family. She also "just for the fun of it" wanted to use the old traditional method of marking the border quilting designs with a teacup.

This delightful winner took top prizes at the Racine County Fair and the Prairie Heritage Quilt Show. Geneva gave it to her daughter on her first wedding anniversary, and the couple have used it every day since then.

Although she is a self-taught quilter, she works continuously at improving her craft, doing much reading and research, attending sympo-

176

siums, workshops, and lectures. She now teaches and has begun judging quilt contests. Since 1977 she has made thirteen full-sized quilts (not including one currently "in the frame," and one top as yet unquilted) as well as ten crib quilts, wall hangings, and large banners.

Many of her quilts have been family efforts, with her husband, daughter, mother-in-law, and son helping in the cutting, sorting, and design arrangement.

MATERIALS

3 yards, approximately, assorted colors of cotton
8 yards white cotton
Dacron-polyester batting

CUTTING GUIDE

This quilt is made of 48 pieced blocks (figures A, B, C, D, and E), surrounded by 28 half-blocks (figures D, E, and F) on sides and ends, and 4 quarter-blocks (figures D, E, and F) at the corners. The inner border, which is 3½″ wide, is made of strips of the white background fabric. The outer border, approximately 3½″ wide, is pieced in the Flying Geese pattern (figures A and G).

Make a stitching template the exact size of each piece and a cutting template the same size plus ¼″ on all edges for seams. (Templates A–G *include* ¼″ seam allowance.) Arrows indicate the straight of grain. Mark templates on the back side of fabric, which has been washed and had the selvage removed. You will need to cut the following:

Figure A–384 assorted colors of cotton for center blocks
Figure B–96 white cotton for center blocks
Figure C–96 white cotton for center blocks
Figure D–140 assorted colors of cotton for center blocks
Figure D-reversed–140 assorted colors of cotton for center blocks
Figure E–140 white cotton for center blocks
Figure E-reversed–140 white cotton for center blocks
Figure F–32 white cotton for half-blocks
Figure F-reversed–32 white cotton for half-blocks
Figure G–approximately 400 white cotton for Flying Geese border
Figure A–approximately 200 assorted colors of cotton for Flying Geese border

ASSEMBLY

To make center block, join 1 piece each from figures A, B, D, and E. Lay aside. Join 1 piece each from figures A, C, D-reversed, and E-reversed. Sew these 2 units together to form one quarter of a block. Repeat 3 times, and join the 4 quarters together with pieces from figure A at center to make 1 block. Piece 48 blocks in this manner. To make the half-blocks, join 1 piece each from figures E, D, and F. Lay aside. Join 1 piece each from figures E-reversed, D-reversed, and F-reversed. Sew these 2 units together with pieces from figure E at center to make 1 half-block.

Piece 8 horizontal strips composed of 1 half-block, 6 blocks, and another half-block. Join the 8 strips together. Piece 2 strips of one quarter-block, 6 half-blocks and another quarter-block. Join 1 of the 2 strips to the top of the 8 strips, the other to the bottom, to make the center of the quilt.

For the inner border, cut 2 strips 4″ × 68″ and 2 strips 4″ × 80″ of white cotton. Sew the longer strips to the sides of center section, and the shorter strips to the top and bottom of the center section.

For Flying Geese border, join 2 pieces from figure G to opposite sides of 1 piece from figure A to form a rectangle. Make as many rectangles as are needed to border quilt, approximately 200. Join the rectangles to form borders of Flying Geese with the geese pointing to the center of each side. To finish corners cut 8 right triangles 3½″. Attach in pairs to form a 3½″ square.

Make quilt back by cutting 2 lengths of white 45″ fabric equal to the length of the quilt plus 3″ (approx-imately 100″). Split 1 piece lengthwise and sew to sides of other piece, so widest section runs down middle of quilt. Excess fabric can be trimmed from edges, leaving approximately 80″ in width.

Assemble the backing, batting, and quilt top. Baste securely from center to corners and then to center of edges. Add more basting to hold securely. Pieced areas are outline-quilted ¼″ from all seams, and strips are quilted with overlapping circles, which may be traced from a teacup or wineglass. Trim edges evenly, and bind with double bias cut from remaining white fabric.

The finished quilt measures 77″ × 97″.

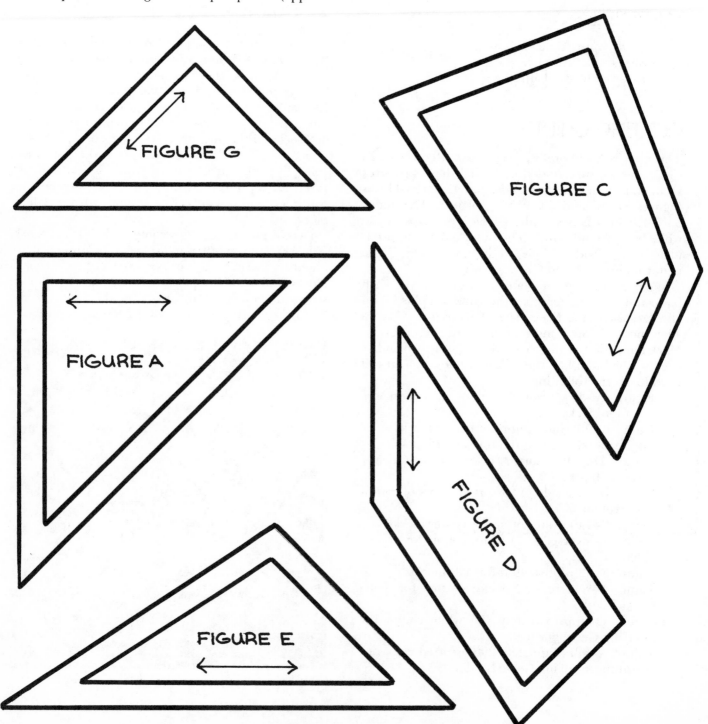

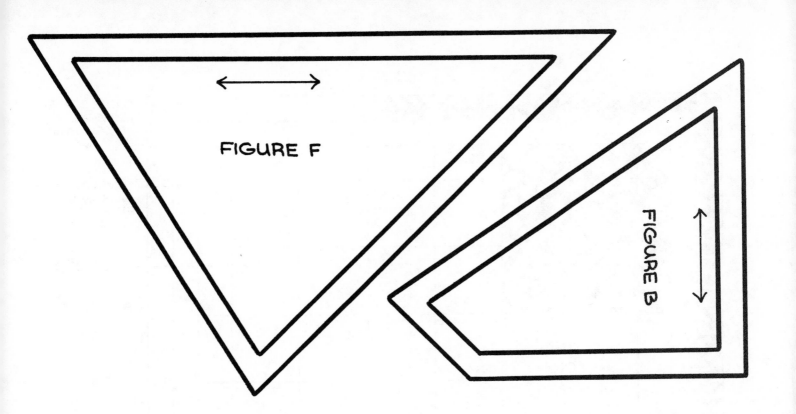

FIGURE F

FIGURE B

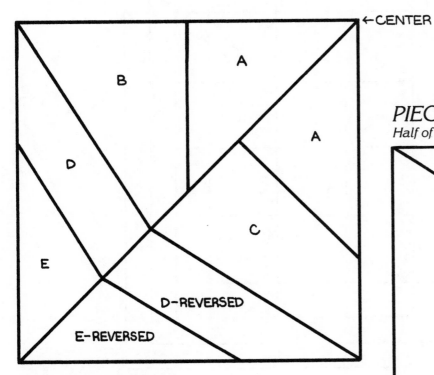

←CENTER

B

A

A

D

C

E

D-REVERSED

E-REVERSED

PIECING GUIDE
One-Quarter of a Block

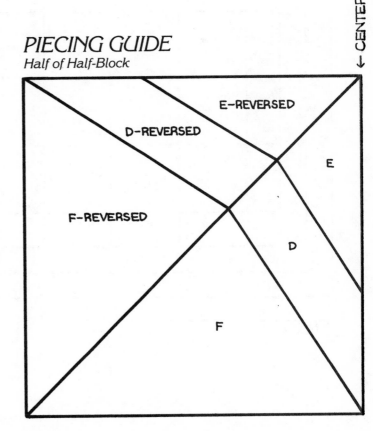

PIECING GUIDE
Half of Half-Block

← CENTER

E-REVERSED

D-REVERSED

E

F-REVERSED

D

F

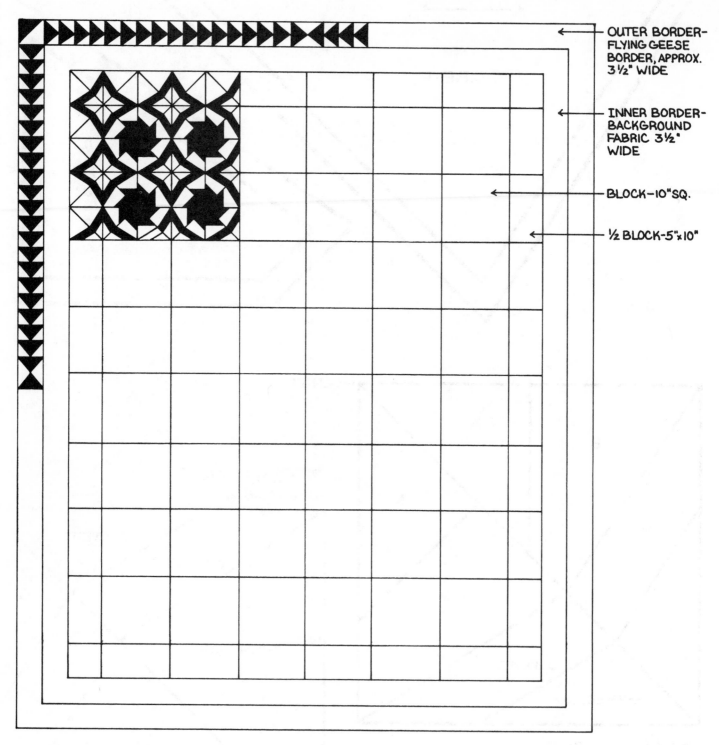

OUTER BORDER-
FLYING GEESE
BORDER, APPROX.
3½" WIDE

INNER BORDER-
BACKGROUND
FABRIC 3½"
WIDE

BLOCK–10"SQ.

½ BLOCK–5"x10"

PIECING GUIDE

180

RADAWN RUUD · *Afton, Wyoming*

BLACK QUILT

C atching up with RaDawn Ruud is no simple matter; she is always on the go. She keeps busy with her husband and two sons, works on the ambulance in her home town, and is always involved in some kind of athletics —softball, volleyball, golf, or swimming. She jokingly tells her friends, "not to tell anyone about the quilting . . . it will blow my image."

Quilting is a family tradition, and RaDawn's mother taught her and her four sisters to quilt when they were very young. RaDawn has been quilting off and on since she was six years old. Her mother, sister, and a friend helped with this quilt, just as she has quilted for them on their projects.

RaDawn's quilts have won First Prize in local county fairs as well as the Wyoming State Fair, with one prizewinner competing against 450 entries.

RaDawn names her quilts herself, choosing the designs especially for the intricate quilting they require. For **Black Quilt**, *she uses tricot fabric for the rich look and satiny feel. She usually uses two-pound Dacron or semi-bonded batting.*

BIBLIOGRAPHY

Bacon, Lenice Ingram. *American Patchwork Quilts*. New York: Bonanza Books, 1980.

Bishop, Robert, William Secord, and Judith Reiter Weissman. *Quilts, Coverlets, Rugs and Samplers*. New York: Alfred A. Knopf, 1982.

Cooper, Patricia, and Norma Bradley Buferd. *The Quilters*. New York: Doubleday & Company, 1977.

Davison, Mildred. *American Quilts from the Art Institute of Chicago*. The Art Institute of Chicago, 1966.

Gutcheon, Beth. *The Perfect Patchwork Primer*. New York: David McKay Company, Inc., 1973.

Ickis, Marguerite. *The Standard Book of Quilt Making and Collecting*. New York: Dover Publications, 1949.

Johnson, Bruce. *A Child's Comfort: Baby and Doll Quilts in American Folk Art*. New York: Harcourt Brace Jovanovich, in association with the Museum of American Folk Art, 1977.

Jones, Stella M. *Hawaiian Quilts*. Honolulu, Hawaii: Daughters of Hawaii and Honolulu Academy of Arts and Mission Houses Museum, 1973.

Kakalia, Kepola U. *Hawaiian Quilting as an Art*. Honolulu, Hawaii, 1976. Deborah Kakalia, Honolulu.

Lithgow, Marilyn. *Quiltmaking and Quiltmakers*. New York: Funk & Wagnalls, 1974.

Mailand, Harold F. *Considerations for the Care of Textiles and Costumes, A Handbook for the Non-Specialist*. Indianapolis, Indiana: Indianapolis Museum of Art, 1980.

McKim, Ruby. *101 Patchwork Patterns*. New York: Dover, 1962.

Murwin, Susan Aylsworth, and Suzzy Chalfant Payne. *Quick and Easy Patchwork on the Sewing Machine*. New York: Dover Publications, 1979.

Orlofsky, Patsy and Myron. *Quilts in America*. New York: McGraw-Hill, 1974.

Payne, Suzzy Chalfant, and Susan Aylsworth Murwin. *Creative American Quilting, Inspired by the Bible*. Old Tappan, New Jersey: Fleming H. Revell Company, 1983.

Wahlman, Maude Southwell. *The Art of Afro-American Quiltmaking*. Bloomington, Indiana: Indiana University Press, 1984.

Walker, Michele. *Quilting and Patchwork*. New York: Ballantine Books, 1983.

Wiebusch, Marguerite. *Feathers and Other Fancies* (quilting patterns). Russiaville, Indiana, 1982.

INDEX

QUILTING RESOURCES

American Quilt Study Group
105 Molino Avenue
Mill Valley, California 94941
A nationwide group interested in the serious study of the history of quilts and textiles, and the women who have made them.

The Continental Quilting Congress, Inc.
P.O. Box 561
Vienna, Virginia 22180

The Embroiderers' Guild of America
6 East 45th Street
New York, New York 10017

National Quilting Association, Inc.
P.O. Box 62
Green Belt, Maryland 20770

Quilters' Journal
P.O. Box 270
Mill Valley, California 94942

PHOTO CREDITS